I AM GHOST HUNTER

By Brad Mikulka

PublishAmerica
Baltimore

ISBN: 1-60610-497-7
PUBLISHED BY PUBLISHAMERICA, LLLP
www.publishamerica.com
Baltimore

Printed in the United States of America

Dedication...

To Brenda for putting up with me...
Thanks to our children Jessica and Sammy for not putting up a
fight because they had to spend another night at grandma's while
mom and dad went on an investigation...

This book is also dedicated to all ghost hunters past, present, and
future. Hope you find your elusive spirits and hopefully you get
them on film or video for the whole world to see.

Introduction

Who, or what, is the SouthEast Michigan Ghost Hunters Society (hence to be known as SEMGHS) you ask, good question. Before I answer that, let me take you back a few years for a little history of the group. It was founded about 12 years ago by a gentleman named Bill Rhodes. Bill was from the Detroit area, hence the name of the group. Back then, the group had a few members, and they did investigations in local cemeteries. I believe it was strictly for fun, just like minded individuals getting together to share a common interest. In 1995, I was at work, surfing the Internet. I had always had an interest in ghosts, more on that later, and I happened upon his group. What I liked about his group was the fact that you didn't have to be a doctor, nor have a PHD in anything to be a member. Just your average "Joe" could join. So I filled out the online application, and became a member. I never went on an actual investigation with Bill. Right after I joined, Bill sent out an e-mail stating that he was moving back to Illinois. He asked if anyone wanted to take over the group, maintain the web site, and such. Being naïve as I was, I eagerly volunteered. Boy, I didn't know what I was getting myself into. After Bill sent me the web pages, I realized something very important; I knew absolutely nothing about what I was doing. I knew nothing about HTML, the language used on web pages; let alone how to maintain the site. We had no equipment, and no idea how to run a group like this, and it is still a learning process. I started out doing this alone. But I recruited my wife Brenda to join, and she has since become Co-Director. She also has the duties of writing up the written report for the clients, and she will sometimes do some of our customer relations duties. Where do I start? First we needed to get some equipment. We had a 35MM camera, so we went out and bought a RCA Camcorder. Here's where my inexperience comes into view. The camcorder was a nice one, but had no external lights to it. After dark, this was totally useless. That's a problem since we do most of our better work after dark. Being your average middle class American, we had to make do until we could afford better equipment. I will not bore you with each piece of equipment that we have acquired over the years, and quite frankly, it would not be interesting reading. But I felt that it was important that you to see how we started in the early days and what we started with. Like the group under Bill, we started out doing cemeteries also. This was mainly because we lacked the equipment, and more importantly, the experience. Getting to investigate a home, is a lot like getting credit. You need credit to get credit, but you can't get credit until you already have credit. This is a catch 22 situation.

Jump ahead to present time. In 2008, we will be celebrating our 12th anniversary. Where has the time gone? Let's just say that we have spent a small fortune on it, or as Brenda is fond of saying the money we spent on the equipment was suppose to go towards the new dining room table. We have done hundred's of investigations, and have been featured on both radio and TV, as well as in print. We have seen members come and go. They either lost interest, or just been busy in normal everyday things. We have the group set up internally like a corporation would. We have a Board of Directors, Trustees, and area reps. The reps responsibility is to contact the client and set up the investigation, and act as a liaison between the home (business) owner and the group. We also have a client, media, and member's handbooks. Some members have complained that we don't need a handbook. I have heard that there are too many rules and restrictions. It has been my experience that you need some kind of guidelines. If you don't, you have organized chaos.

We never intended on writing a book when we started. But, for reasons unknown, the time just seems right. Is there maybe some divine intervention? Maybe, but we will probably never know.

Who We Are

Since we have given you a basic introduction of how the group came to be, let's take a few minutes to answer the burning question about what we do. As the name implies, we hunt ghosts. Well, not exactly. We are asked to investigate homes or business where they are experiencing activity. But unlike our counterparts in the movie "Ghostbusters," the movie of a few years back, we do not have the capability to catch and store the ghosts, and we don't drive a hearse (it's in the shop for repairs). But seriously, what we do is quite simple: We help people that might have a spirit or two in their house. First off, I don't like the word "ghosts." That word is the image that Hollywood projects to sell movies. And when most people hear the word ghosts you generally get the impression of a white sheet floating around and scarring people or a dead person's spirit seeking revenge for their death. So from this point forward they will be referred to as spirits. The spirits were at one time a father or mother, brother or sister, or a good friend. Heck, it could have been your dog Fido. And for some reason they are still stuck here on earth. Most of the time we are asked to figure out who is there causing the activity. Occasionally, we are asked to help the spirit "cross" over, so to speak, which we have had success with over the years. It generally involves holy water, prayer, and incense. We would not recommend people try this if they are inexperienced. You may cause more harm than good. The group itself encompasses a wide range of ages and occupations. We have members in age from 18-60 and office managers to State workers. As in the original founder's guidelines all membership in the group is free of charge. We feel that you shouldn't have to pay to learn how to be a ghost hunter. There are no monthly dues, fees to pay, or hidden costs. The only time that you will be asked to pay is for those special times when we need to pay or make a donation to gain access to an investigation.

We do, however, have T-shirts for sale. We don't make a profit from the sale, but we want the group to look as professional as possible. The purchase of the shirts is optional, but encouraged if you plan on attending investigations with us.

Just a final thought about who we are. The members of SEMGHS are generally everyday, down to earth people. Some have special abilities, most don't. But that is what makes the group so great, in my opinion. No one gets special treatment in the group. Everyone is welcomed with open arms and is treated as equals. Some members have lived in haunted houses before so they can relate to what the homeowners are experiencing. Granted, not all hauntings are the same and they might not be having the same problems as you are but they can relate and that is what's important.

Our Better Investigations over Ten Years

The rest of this book covers some of our investigations that we have conducted over the last 12 years. I will not name names, locations of the investigations, for obvious reasons. We don't want people driving by the houses or staking them out. Or worse yet, calling or going to the front door asking to come in or to take pictures. I know that it is fun to read about haunted houses and such, so I hope you enjoy them as much as we had enjoyed doing the investigation. Just one final thought on all of this. People always ask us this, "If you come out and don't get anything, does it mean my house isn't haunted?" NO, it doesn't. Some groups want you to believe that if they don't find anything the place isn't haunted. Not true. It just might be that the spirits were not active during the investigation and just because we didn't find anything doesn't mean that there wasn't anything there. For what ever reason the spirits didn't want to show themselves to us during the time we spent there. The people that live in the house are there much more than we are. We only have 4 hours in the house. Unless we spent as much time as they do in the house we can't say for 100% whether or not there are any spirits in the house. You will find no cute indications of activity here. There will be no 3 out of 5 stars here or any of those cutesy haunting graphs there. We will however offer a conclusion after each investigation. This is solely for offering our thoughts on whether or not the place that we had just investigated has activity in it. We don't believe in making fun of people who are living with spirits, even if they are subtle. Plus we feel that it takes the seriousness out of the situation and makes it appear that we don't care for our clients, which isn't the case.

Where's the Cat??

Date: 06-15-00
Location: Cemetery near Lansing, MI

Back in the day when all we did investigation wise were cemeteries, this one sticks out as one of the better ones. We had been to this particular cemetery a few years before this investigation. During that visit, attended by a whopping two of us, we caught something on video that we can't explain. Back then though our video camera was the kind that was really heavy, bulky, and didn't have any external lights. So in layman's terms, when the sun went down, our video capabilities were poor at best. But we did get an orb on video. Even in total darkness, the orb had a self illumination where it could be seen.

During the first visit to the cemetery, my cousin Marc and I were the only two members who were brave enough, or dumb enough, to attend this investigation. You have to admit that this is not something that the average person does. Most people do whatever they can to avoid cemeteries, and most people that I know would not be caught dead, no pun intended, in a cemetery after dark.

There I go again, wandering off the subject. Let's get back to the first trip at the cemetery. The sun had gone down and it was getting really dark by that time. Marc and I had wandered off towards a few of the bigger monuments in this cemetery when one in particular caught our attention. There were two tall monuments standing side by side and they happened to be facing towards the west. With the video camera that we had then, like I mentioned, didn't have external lights. So we were using what little light there was left coming from the horizon as light for the camera. Marc had the camera on his shoulder for most of the night and it was getting pretty heavy at that point. So he dropped it down and held it by the handle about knee high. It was facing the twin monuments. We didn't see anything at the time but saw something pretty interesting when we reviewed the tape when we got home. Most of the time you don't see the orbs with your own eyes, it is only during playback of the tape that you see them. It has something to do with the spectrum of light that we can't see and the chemicals used on the tapes.

We came back home around 9:45-10:00 PM and talked for awhile about the cemetery. Marc left around 10:45 PM and I didn't get a chance to look at the film that night. We had two young children at the time and anyone with young children knows that you have almost zero free time. I didn't get to the video tape for almost a week after the investigation.

What we saw was pretty amazing. The video starts out with daylight and everything could be seen on the video tape, including bugs whizzing by that are sometimes mistaken as orbs. Then the sun starts setting and the cemetery starts to get dark and even more bugs come out and flying by the camera. Just a word of note; always use bug spray when outside and in Michigan during the summer months. We wandered around for the next hour, making small talk. We didn't see anything with the video camera or for that matter anywhere else. We then walked over to the twin monuments and commented about how cool they looked. The light was gone now, and the camera would focus in and out whenever it would detect movement. This is caused by the auto focus on the camera "seeing" something that we can't and trying to focus on this object.

A few minutes after we stopped at the twin monuments, you can hear Marc comment, and you could hear his voice on the video tape, on how heavy the camera was and that he was going to keep recording but was taking the camera off his shoulder and was going to carry it by the handle instead. The view changes, now the video camera is about knee high looking directly in front of us, as we continue to talk. Then directly in front of us, about 1 foot away, was a moving, glowing ball of light. It seemed to have come from behind us, zig zagged as it went away from us, and then disappeared as it moved away from us, no more than 10 feet away. The amazing part, other than what was on video, was the fact that we didn't see anything with our eyes. We saw nothing when we were there in the cemetery. It wasn't until we got home and watched the video that the object appeared in front of us. It was as if whatever it was came to check us out and see what was happening.

People that have seen the video have written the object off as either a bug or dust, but no one has said anything about it possibility being something supernatural. Okay, it wasn't a bug. No ifs or butts about it. The thing was too big, too round, and glowed. If it was a bug, maybe a lightning bug, it was the biggest bug I have ever seen and the brightest bug I have ever seen. Whatever it was stayed illuminated the whole time it was in view on the tape. I have never personally seen a lightening bug stay this bright for so long. And dust? No way. If it was a particle of dust, it could have hurt someone if it hit someone, this thing was that big. You have to remember. Our video camera didn't have any external lights, none. We had no flashlights on at the time, and the cemetery was in the middle of nowhere. There were no lights around for miles, not even street lights. To this day I believe it was a spirit orb.

I didn't mean to be so long winded on that story; I haven't even gotten to the good one yet. Not saying that the orb story wasn't good but I think that this one is a little bit better.

We did another investigation at the same cemetery a few years later. This time around we had a total of four members present and a little more equipment. We even had video cameras this time that could record in total darkness, a big jump in technology that we had even a few years earlier. The night was warm. There was a little breeze, and a full moon. This would give us a little more light to see by. And every little bit helps.

Like I said before, this cemetery is in the middle of the boonies. It takes about 30 minutes from our house in Lansing to get there. We arrived a little after 8PM. This time of year, the sun doesn't set until 9:30PM or so, and this would give us plenty of time to walk around and get a feel for the place before we set up our equipment.

We did a complete walk around of the cemetery, and to be honest, there wasn't any particular place that reached out and grabbed us. The reason that you do a walk around is mainly for two things. First off, it lets the spirits know your intentions, and secondly, it allows you to get a feel for the place and lets you determine the spots that might produce some activity. Just because the area doesn't seem like it will be active doesn't necessarily mean that it will stay that way during the investigation. Places can get active real quick, where a few minutes earlier the same area was totally dead, no pun intended.

We found two places that had trace EMF readings and small temperature changes so we set up one video camera in each of those areas. We also put motion detectors in each area. These are handy little devices because they allow you to monitor any area for movement but they also give you the freedom to wander away from these areas. The annoying sounds they omit will alert you to movement they pick up and will allow you to rush back to the area and see what set them off. This would be a good time to remind you that any movement will set these motion detectors off, even live people, so before you break your neck tripping over gravestones in your rush to get to the area that the motion detectors are set up, make sure that other members of your team didn't set them off. It will save you a lot of running around, trust me. We have our members say something like "It was me" if they set them off. Try it; you will save wear and tear on the sneakers.

Once you have your equipment set up there isn't much to do except either sit there by them and watch, or you can wander around. In our case we decided to walk around the cemetery that wasn't being watched by the video cameras. We still had digital cameras with us so if anything did happen we would be sure to get it on film. We didn't take any pictures of what happened next because it was just something that happens everyday, usually not in cemeteries and not in the waning hours of the day, and we honestly didn't think twice about it.

Like most cemeteries, this particular one had a path, for lack of a better name, where cars and yes, even the hearse, could drive in and out of the cemetery. We had two members at the far end of this road, on the far end of the cemetery. Another member and I were walking on the path towards the other members. There were tombstones on either side of us and up ahead on the right was a big bush. This plant was on a slight incline. I don't know if this would classify as a flower. It was big, round, but only a few feet high. We could easily see either side of the bush clearly. We were approximately 20 feet away from this bush, when on the other side was a black cat. I know the lure of black cats and witches and cemeteries, but I swear this was a black cat. It was sitting on all fours and looking away from us. We were walking towards the cat and making a noise on the path but the cat acted like we weren't even there, or maybe the cat wasn't of this earth. It didn't move, didn't even look back at us. I don't know about you, but whenever I have walked towards a cat it always runs away before I can even get close to it. I remember even commenting to the other member with me that it was strange that the cat hadn't even moved even though we were getting close to it.

I had even made a smart-alecky remark that it might even be a ghost cat. How right I was. As we got within a few feet of the bush, the cat was gone. It just vanished. It was literally there one second and gone the next. The other members were just a few feet away from us now and we asked them where the cat went. They had a clear view of the whole area and didn't even see the cat! This proves that not everyone sees the same thing at the same time. We had two members that had seen the cat for a couple of minutes and we had two members that were closer to the area than we were, and they had seen no trace of the black cat.

So we had to tell them that we had watched the cat as we walked up the path and just before we reached the bush, it was gone. Again the thing that sticks our in my mind was the fact that the cat didn't move and that as we got closer to it, it never acknowledged that we were even there.

Conclusion: Did we see a ghost cat? Yes, to this very day I swear that we did. But this raises a couple of questions. Was the cat buried in the cemetery or was it just waiting for its owner to return to it. We never even thought about it at the time but we should have checked the tombstones in the area near where the cat was and see what we could find. Without having names that would be like trying to find the preverbal needle in a haystack.

A Tragedy in a Small Town...

Date: Numerous visits
Location: Bath, Michigan

You wouldn't think that a small town could be the site of an unspeakable horror, but this is what happened to the little town of Bath, Michigan on May 18, 1927. They were an unwilling participatant in the horror that happened. Bath Michigan is approximately 10 miles northeast of the capital city of Lansing. There is nothing that would normally set this town apart from any other small Midwestern town. Most of the business's that were once thriving are now long gone, having moved to the bigger cities. There are only a few businesses still in Bath. The town doesn't even have a stoplight. Now days, families come and go and they don't know the history of what happened. In 1927 however, everyone knew each other. So the pain felt by one family was felt literally by the whole town. And on this day, the whole town was hurting.

So what exactly happened you ask? There are even some people in the Mid-Michigan area that don't know what happened on that fateful day. I will admit that even I didn't know what had happened until a few years ago. And I was born and raised in the area. What happened in this small town is today still the deadliest school attack in the United States. On May 18, 1927, a local farmer blew up the Bath Consolidated School. The tragic event took 45 lives, 38 of these being children. There have been numerous books written about this so I will not go too deep into the story but I feel that you need to know a little about the "why's" so I will attempt to give some insight of what transpired years ago that caused the local man to do what he did to the school.

Andrew Kehoe came to Bath in the spring of 1919. He had a nice house approximately one mile east of town. As a farmer he started to experiment with dynamite to clear stumps from his farm land. He then started using watches to use as timers in coordination with the dynamite. He then could control when the dynamite went off. The house is no longer there since he burned it down before he killed himself. Oh, by the way he killed his wife also. They found her body in a wheelbarrow near where the barn once stood. They looked for her for days before they finally found her body. Not only did he burn down the house, he also burned all of his farm buildings. And just for good measures, before he burned down his barn he tied the legs of his horses together with wire so they couldn't escape. To no one's surprise the horses also died in the fire.

Back to the story, albeit it is a condensed one. Kehoe served on the school board and was the treasurer for a few years. Before the decision was made to consolidate the Bath schools, many one and two room school houses dotted the area countryside. The new school would eliminate the need for the country schools and the new consolidated school would hold grades K-12 in one building. When they built the new school, they also raised the taxes. Kehoe fell behind in his taxes and he was going to lose his farm. The ironic thing was that he would have had enough money to pay his back taxes if he would have sold all of his farm equipment. But then again if he had sold off all of his farm equipment, how would he be able to farm the land. He had an ongoing feud with the superintendent of the schools. A gentleman named Emory Huyck. Mr. Huyck and Kehoe never got along. If Huyck suggested a new bus driver Kehoe objected. If they wanted to give the teachers longer vacations, Kehoe objected. Basically whatever they wanted to do, Kehoe didn't. The feud between Huyck and Kehoe went on for years. The school board had no idea of the intentions of Kehoe. The school was looking for a new maintenance man, and when Kehoe offered to be the maintenance man for the school they jumped at the chance and gave him the job. They figured they could save a few dollars by giving Kehoe the job instead of hiring a perfect stranger. His job responsibilities included general maintenance on the school and to make sure that the boilers were in good repair. This new job gave him access to the school whenever he wanted and no one in the town gave it a second thought when he was there after school hours. The townspeople thought that he was there working in the basement on the boilers when in reality he was rigging the basement with hundreds of pounds of explosives, using watches as timers to set off the dynamite on the last day of school. After the bombing, they had interviewed a woman that lived right next to the school. She said that she had seen Kehoe going into the school late at night but she didn't think anything of it. She saw him go between the school and his truck many times and thought that he was bringing in tools to work on things.

The day of the bombing, May 18th, 1927 was the last day of the school year. The seniors were in the church next door practicing for graduation. The rest of the students were in the school taking final exams. In a recent interview with a local paper, one of the survivors told of seeing Kehoe standing near the bus as the students came off the bus. Kehoe told them "This is your last day boys." The survivors were quoted as saying that they thought he was talking about the last day of school, not the last day of their lives. This statement was about to come true for 38 of the children that day.

Even though the man was evil, you have to give him some credit for the way he thought this whole thing out. First he set off dynamite at his house. The resulting explosion and fire was seen and felt for many miles. The residents of Bath and his neighbors all came to his aid. This at the time was not uncommon. When they were enroute to Kehoe's house the dynamite at the school went off. The townspeople then had to do an about face and then rush back into town to see what the explosion there was. He had them going in one direction and then made them go the opposite way.

Everyone in town came to the aid of the school after the bombs went off. Word was sent to local towns that the town of Bath needed help, and to come as fast as you could. Help came in the form of police, doctors, and ambulances. Also, the press came. The school bombing made front page news in the entire country.

Nearly everyone in the town was affected by this event. Family's lost one or two children and it was said that someone knew someone in town that lost a child. It took years for the town to recover and some families never have.

In a sad ironic fate, after the bombing Kehoe drove past the school and noticed that the school was still standing. Obliviously things didn't go as planned as the school was still standing. So Kehoe circled around the block and went back past his house. He continued into town and made the turn onto Main Street. He stopped a few houses short of the school and noticed that Huyck was standing nearby and called him over. No one will ever know why he did this but it might be safe to say that Kehoe wanted to finish the feud he had with Huyck. Following Huyck was the postmaster, a retired farmer who had come to help, and a student that survived the bombing. What they didn't know was that Kehoe had loaded the back of his Model T with dynamite and embedded it with nails and pieces of steel. When they were right next to the car, Kehoe grabbed the shotgun he had in the front seat, aimed it at the back seat, and pulled the trigger.

The resulting explosion sent people running for cover. Innocent people on the street were hit by the steel and nails. People thought that there was another explosion at the school. This was right after WWI and people actually thought that the Germans had came over here and planted explosives in the power lines and that they were going off.

What happened to Huyck, the postmaster, the farmer, and the student? They all were killed by the explosion. Kehoe was killed also. The only way they were able to identify his remains was because they found his ID in his pants pocket of what was left of his body. It was said that his intestines were hanging from the nearby power lines.

That's all I am going to say about the cause of the bombing. I don't think we need to talk about the injuries caused and the scars that never healed. I am no expert about the bombing, not by any means. There are books about the bombings and when we first learned of the site, I strongly believed that I should know as much as I could about the cause and effect of the tragedy. I wanted to learn as much as I could about the site before we did an investigation there.

Now we are at the stage where I can tell you about some of the things that we have experienced while investigating the Bath School bombing site. We have been there numerous times, so I will not tell you about each and every one. That would be boring to you to read because we didn't get activity each time we were there, and as you get older they say that your memory is the first to go. Well mine isn't gone yet, but it is hard for me to remember each and every time we were there and every occurrence that didn't stand out as being different from the others. I will however, relate to you the things that have stuck out in my mind as being the better experiences of the park, I hope that you will agree.

During one of our first times to the park the bell tower proved to be the focal point for some really strong activity. The bell tower is the only thing left of the original school and is nearly in the center of the park. We had put up two motion detectors around the bell tower, one was on the left side, and the other one was placed directly across from the first one, but was placed on the other side of the bell tower.

They were placed so they were not in direct line of each other. We also had a tape recorder on the same bench as the motion detector and made sure it was recording. Both of the books that we have about the bombing have the names of both the survivors and victims of the tragic event. So we thought what if we stood near the bell tower, and read off the names of the kids that were killed as if we were the teachers and we were taking morning attendance. If the spirits of the children were indeed there, this experiment just might make them come to us and hopefully make their presence known to us.

That is exactly what we did. We made sure to stand behind the front motion detector as not to set it off, and we started to read the names of the children who did not survive the bombing. We paused between each name, in an attempt to get some EVP. We have learned to pause for between 4-5 breaths between each question when we are doing an EVP session. We have found that this gives the spirit time to answer without us cutting him/her off or inadvertently talking over him/her when we ask the next question.

We made it through the first 10 or so names without any incident. Not even the slightest thing happened to reward our efforts. There is something strange about the park that I must mention though before I continue. It seems that Kehoe, the "mad bomber" as he was called in the day, always seems to make an appearance in the park around 9:30 PM, at least his spirit does. At least this is what we have learned over the years of coming to the park. Almost every time around then, the wind picks up, it is noticeably colder, and the spirits of the children seem to all vanish from the park, as if they are still trying to hide from him, 80 years after the bombing. You can feel Kehoe's spirit until 10:00 PM, and then all is quiet. No more activity, the temperature rises back up to the surrounding area, and all of our equipment goes silent. No EMF, nothing shows up when we take pictures. It is as if someone flicks a switch and everything just stops.

You have to experience it to really believe it. You can almost set your watch by this.

Like I said, we had no luck at all for the first few names. But we continued to read the names in hopes that something would get awoken and make the night interesting. We didn't know how interesting things would be getting real soon.

We read a few more names without incident when the motion detector farthest away from us went off. Then a few seconds later the front motion detector, the one right in front of us went off also. Whatever was setting these off was moving in a circle around the bell tower in a counterclockwise motion. We looked at our watches; it was 9:27 PM. Looks like Kehoe was arriving a little early tonight and that was perfectly fine with us.

Sure enough, right after the motion detectors went off the wind started to pick and we recorded a temperature drop of 10 degrees in less than 3 minutes. The cold seemed to be centered on the bell tower. Then just as quickly as everything seemed to pick up, nothing. The temperature slowly rose to where it was before this started. The air was still, none of the motion detectors were going off. I think the worse thing that happened was that we were not ready or prepared to take pictures. We didn't document any of this. So this just goes to show you that you need to be prepared all the time in case something like this was to happen. I would bet that the spirits are just waiting for the right moment to catch you off guard so they can make a fool out of you. It worked this time, but we were ready for anything that would happen next.

With the excitement from the first wave over, we realized that we had only made it down half the list of the people killed, that we were reading from the book. We thought that if we got this kind of response from reading only half way through the list, we might as well continue until all the names were read. Looking back after the investigation was over I am glad that we did.

We had read 5 more names when, like a repeat from the first activity, the back motion detector went off. Then a few seconds later the front one went off. But unlike the first time, they kept on going off. The back motion detector went off then the front motion detector went off. This continued on for 10 whole cycles. Back, front, back, front and so on, I think you get the picture.

However, unlike the first time, we were more than ready this time for, excuse the pun, anything they threw at us!

While one of our members read the last few names out loud, I was ready with the digital camera. But instead of standing around like I did the first time, I was moving around the bell tower waiting for the motion detectors to go off. I was sure not to get in front of either one of them as I would have set off the motion detectors. I was near the back one when the front one went off, I immediately started taking pictures. Then the front one went off. So I ran towards that one, stopping every few seconds to snap off a few pictures. Then the back one went off again. Whatever it was it was literally running circles around me, and tiring me out in the process. I was getting dizzy from running around in circles. It seemed like forever, but the whole thing lasted no more than 2 minutes tops.

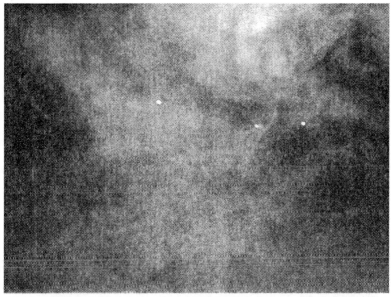

Ectoplasmic Mist near the bell tower at the Bath school bombing site during a SEMGHS investigation.

Again all was quiet. The temperature was rising, no EMF, and the motion detectors were again silent. I was still ready to take pictures if anything happened, but I stopped for a few minutes to see the pictures I had taken on the digital camera. I was amazed at what I had got. There on the camera was some of the best ectoplasmic mist I had ever seen. They appeared as massive streaks around the bell tower. The mist looked like whatever or whoever it might have been was running around the bell tower at the same time I was taking the pictures. This would be evidence that the motion detectors were doing their job and that they do indeed pick up anything that we can or can't see. The night was a success in our eyes. We had some good pictures and a good time was had by all. We told the "kids" goodnight and that we would see them next year.

Another investigation of interest happened a few years later. We had an unusually large group for this investigation. Since the park covers a large area, this usually isn't a problem. And more often than not, many of the people that live near the park will stop by and see what we are doing and whether or not we have found anything. Most of them are cool with what we do. As long as you don't cause trouble and leave at a respectable time, they have no trouble with us being there. We have had our share of run ins with people that don't believe in this stuff and think we are all morbid for being in a place where so many people died. That happens, not everyone thinks the same way as everyone does. As the old saying goes, you can't please everyone all of the time

When we have this many new members attending an investigation at the bombing site we like to give them a little history lesson about the place. I don't like to just show up and start the investigation. So on this occasion we met first at the local cemetery where some of the victims are buried. I did some research before hand and found where some of the people were buried, by this I mean their exact location in the cemetery and if possible, pictures of the tombstones. We met at a local restaurant, and after a quick but satisfying meal, we started to the cemetery. We arrived after a short drive, and proceeded to the very back right corner of the cemetery. Once we all gathered in a small circle, I thanked them for coming to this investigation and gave a little speech of why we were in the cemetery and what happened at the bombing site. Just a little orientation of what happened here years ago.

I then whipped out my little book about the bombing and read a little about each victim. Their likes, what happened on the day of the bombing, and whether or not they perished on that day. If they did pass because of the bombing, I took out my other map and took them to their tombstone and then I read the name on the tombstone. My audience had shocked looks on their faces. It is one thing to be doing investigations in homes or trampling through cemeteries not knowing who used to live there or what haunts the place. It is an entirely different feeling when you can put a face to the tombstones and you know how they met their fate.

We were there on the actual anniversary so they had a ceremony there in the morning and a fresh wreath of flowers was placed next to the bell tower. I would have liked to been there but having kids and a job, I couldn't attend. I encouraged the new members to walk around the park to get a feel for the area and maybe take what I read them from the book and try to imagine what it was like on that day in 1927. That day the seniors were in the church next door practicing for graduation. The younger kids were in school taking exams. It was a fine spring day, May 18, 1927.

The investigation was like any normal ones at the park. Getting just enough activity to keep us there but nothing to say "oh my gosh," what was that. We had few younger aged members at this investigation. We were pretty spread out all over the park. We had set up a video camera, EMF meter, and motion detector by the bell tower. We had another video camera by the church. We had some members trying to find a quiet spot for EVP's. Others were just walking around taking EMF readings and taking digital pictures. Others were more than happy to sit on the numerous benches in the park and soak up the whole experience.

I was doing what I usually do at investigations, which is going around and helping members with questions, setting up the equipment, only after I do this can I settle down and watch and see what happens.

I was sitting down next to the bell tower, which is my customary spot during investigations at Bath. There were 5-10 members to my right no more than 50 feet away, the wife included, and sitting on the benches facing away from the road. There were a handful of members near the church, which is to my right and about 200 feet away. I had 5 members near the bell tower and the rest were scattered all around the park.

Brenda was the first to approach me with something that she had seen. She said that there was an empty bench right behind them. She and a couple of other members looked that way and there was a man sitting on the bench. He was sitting crossed legged and was dressed in dirty and ratty clothes. He was facing straight ahead and had his eyes closed. He had his arms resting on his legs with his palms facing up. The way you do if you are doing yoga or meditation. Brenda said that he didn't say a word the whole time that they noticed him there. She looked away for a few seconds to say something to another member, and when she looked back at him, he was gone. They looked around quickly to see where he had gone to and they didn't see him around anywhere. They were almost in the center of the park when this happened so the chances of him leaving the park without being seen by someone were slim at best.

Our member, Dennis came to me about 15 minutes later and told me that he had something to tell me and that I probably wouldn't believe him. Dennis is one of the most level headed people I have ever met. He wouldn't make things up just to bring attention to himself.

This is what he told me. He saw the same person that Brenda and the others saw. But he saw him walking towards a group of members near the bell tower. Dennis said that he was between the church and the group of members sitting on the benches. He assumed that the guy was someone that lived near the park and he was afraid that the man was going to confront some of the younger, female members that had gathered near the bell tower since he was walking straight towards them. He didn't want the man to give them any trouble so he started to walk towards the bell tower. The girls moved from the spot just to the right of the bell tower to the other side, out of view of Dennis. The man walked that way and soon he was out of view also. Dennis, still being a good 25 feet away, picked up the pace to catch up to the man and the girls. He said that when he rounded the bell tower the girls were there but the man had disappeared. He asked the girls where the old man was and they looked at him funny and asked "What old man?" Dennis said that he only lost sight of the old man for a few seconds after he was on the other side of the bell tower. But the girls should have seen him because they were standing at the exact spot where the old man was heading. Both the girls and Dennis looked around for the old man but he was no where to be seen. To this day we don't know who he was and how he was connected to the park, if he even was for that matter. Maybe this was the spirit of Kehoe still trying to stir up trouble.

Out of the many times that we have been to the park, these two times were the only two times where something odd happened. You can always count on getting pieces of clothing pulled as if a child were trying to get your attention, many good digital pictures, and the occasional EVP. We will be back again and it is our hope that the children will be there to greet us.

Conclusion- Is the Bath Bombing site haunted? I don't know if I would use the term haunted but we believe that there is something there that we can't explain. It has all the characteristics of what we believe cause a place to be haunted. It has a tragic past so many people lost there lives in a horrific and tragic way, and the raw emotions from the parents and friends alike not knowing if their loved ones were alive or dead. The feeling of the park has changed, it feels different.

Back to School...

Date: 07-10-06
Location: Somewhere in Michigan

When I graduated high school, I swore that I would never go back to school again. Don't get me wrong, I have nothing against higher education. It just isn't for me. Just the thought of spending 2-4 more years in the classroom, cramming for exams, and all the unpleasantness that goes along with it just wasn't my cup of tea.

One of our members, we will use the name Annie to protect the name and location of the school, said that the school her son attends was having activity. Her son had told her things that had happened, as well as the teachers and custodians who are there after everyone has left. They asked us if we would be interested in doing an investigation there. We jumped at the chance because along with nursing homes, hospitals, and funeral homes, schools are really hard to get access to for investigations. The reason is simple. You don't want the stigma that goes along with having a haunted place at work or of higher education. Can you imagine how many people would pull their children out of schools if they thought it was haunted? Some might not, but I would bet many more would.

Next came the nightmare of setting this investigation up. We had to do it when there were no teachers present. Even though some were very interested in being there, at least for the first investigation, as another one is planned in the future, we thought best to have just the investigation team present. We had to coordinate our schedule with the principle since he would be letting us in.

This was going to be a major undertaking just because of the sheer size of the place. We have never done an investigation before in a place of this size. It would put a strain on our resources but it was way too much an opportunity to pass up.

We met before the investigation at a local restaurant. We were to meet the principle, I'll call him Jim, at the school at a pre-specified time and he would let us in, lock the doors, and return at 11 PM to let us out and lock the doors behind us. So we had only 4 hours to conduct an investigation in a building of this size. We obviously couldn't cover all of the building, so when Annie took us through the building, we had her show us the places where activity had been reported and to save time we concentrated only on these areas.

So the areas that we were going to cover were a specific classroom, a hallway next to the gym, and the old locker room behind the gym. As I get to these areas, I will give a brief history of the activity that had been reported.

The first area that we set up in was one of the classrooms. There have been many reported occurrences here so this was one of the areas that we wanted to cover. The classroom is like every other classroom in most schools except for one small exception. It has stairs in the corner that leads up to a small storage area that is above the classroom. You can close the door to the stairs and you wouldn't even know that the stairs were there, you would just assume that there was a closet there.

On one occasion the room was full of students. The teacher was going over a lesson when the closest person to the door noticed that the door knob was turning. It was as if someone was coming down the stairs and wanted into the classroom. There shouldn't have been anyone in the storage room as the teacher hadn't seen anyone go up there. Plus, she always keeps the door locked to discourage any student from wondering off and maybe hurting themselves up in the storage room. After a few seconds, she said that the door knob stopped moving. She assumed that the student had an overactive imagination and didn't think anymore of it. But then again a few minutes later the same student again said that the door knob was moving. This time the teacher saw it move also. She grabbed the keys and went over to the door. The door knob was still moving; again it looked like someone was trying to enter the classroom from the storage room. She quickly unlocked the door, flung the door open, but no one was there. She went up the stairs and did a quick scan but there was not a living soul up there. This door is the only way in or out of the storage room. If there was someone on the other side of the door, there is no place for them to exit except for the door that goes into the classroom.

The same thing happened a few days later, this time however the teacher had came in early to grade some papers and get ready for the day ahead. She was the only one in the classroom that morning. She told us that she was doing some work and heard a jiggling noise coming from the stairwell door leading to the storage room. She went over to the door and again the door knob was moving. She left the room immediately. She said it was one thing to be in a room full of kids when the door knob is moving on its own accord, but it is a totally different situation when she is by herself. That was not something that she was too fond of.

We only had one wireless video camera for this investigation, we now are completely wireless, and so we set it up in this classroom 10 feet from the stairs heading to the storage area. Since the monitor would not work in the gym, the distance is too far, we put the camera in the classroom also. We also set up our Trifield EMF on the stairs as well as a motion detector at the bottom of the stairs on a bookcase, facing up the stairs. If anything came up or down the stairs we would see it on the video monitor and hear it since the motion detector should detect movement on the stairs and sound the alarm.

We stayed in this room for almost the whole investigation. It seemed to be the most active place in the school. Other members came in and went back out, but most of us stayed just in this room. We were in constant contact with each other via 2-way radios. So if anyone needed any person for any reason what so ever, they were only a call away.

We just sat and waited to see if we would have any visitors during the evening. A handful of times we would hear noises like someone was walking on the ceiling. The classroom had a suspended ceiling. The storage room upstairs was over the suspended ceiling but under the main roof of the school. Whenever we heard noises that appeared to be on the suspended ceiling we would try to track them and see where they were heading. There was no way other than lifting the panels on the ceiling, which in hindsight we should have done to see if any animal was making the noises.

I mentioned earlier this happened a handful of times. We took pictures and a few of them appeared to have orbs in them. Towards the end of the investigation we did get an orb on video. We were all sitting there in the classroom when the Trifield EMF on the stairs went off. With the Trifield where it was and where we were sitting we didn't have a clear view of it. So we didn't know what had set it off. A few seconds after the EMF went off the motion detector at the bottom of the stairs went off. This meant to us that whatever it was had mass to set off the motion detectors and it had some kind of energy to set off the EMF meter. We took tons of pictures after this happened but nothing seemed to be on any of our cameras. It wasn't until we reviewed the video days later that we saw what had set off the equipment on the stairs.

The video camera was set up with a side view of the stairs. So you didn't get a direct view up the stairs. On the video tape you could hear the Trifield EMF that was on the steps going off then a few seconds later the motion detector at the bottom of the stairs went off.

Then the orb that had set these off came into view of the camera. The orb, which is a spirit of a person that has passed, had came down the stairs first setting off the Trifield EMF then moved down the stairs and set off the motion detector, then it turned the corner and headed into the classroom. This is when the camera had its first visual of our visitor. The orb just continued a few more first than vanished from sight. That made the whole investigation. You live for these moments. It is one thing to get orbs on pictures. It is another thing to get orbs on video. Skeptics will argue that these little balls of light are just dust particles. To which we will agree to some point most of the orbs caught on video are dust particles. However, the crème de la crème of this particular event is that not only do we have an orb showing intelligence, it came down the stairs and turned the corner on its own accord, but it set off BOTH the Trifield EMF AND the motion detector. This was a good night indeed.

The second place that we set up was the hallway behind the gym. In this hallway there have been reports on feeling cold breezes go past you, dark figures moving in the hallway and a dark figure seen going through the wall from the hallway heading into the gym.

Even though most of the equipment we had was concentrated on the classroom, Charles, our veteran member, had put one of his video cameras on a tripod and placed it in this hallway. Bryan, another member of the group, took some pictures of the hallway. Charles didn't get anything on his video cameras, but Bryan has what looks like to us an apparition at the end off the hall. You can see a human shape, but the figure is transparent.

The last place where we had set up video cameras was the old locker room right off the stage in the gym. There have been reports of the water faucets being turned on by themselves and an apparition of little boy has also been seen in this area.

We put a video camera on a tripod in this area and focused it first on the sink that the water faucet allegedly was turned on while a witness saw this happen right in front of his eyes. We would keep the video camera here for an hour or so then we would move it. We try to move the camera every hour as this helps us from falling asleep when we have hours of video footage to watch at home and it helps that we don't have to look at the same scenery for the whole time.

We came into the room every so often to check on the camera and to make sure it was still recording. It is not uncommon to have the video camera turn off, usually by an unseen hand. This has happened to us a handful of times at previous investigations. We did our checks and everything seemed to be in working order. We didn't have a monitor connected to the camera so we had no idea of what was appearing on the video. The only way was to watch the tapes later. We had moved back to the classroom and it was time for us to move the camera. We radioed to any members that were in the area of the locker room to move the camera to a different part of the room. A couple of members were in the gym, so they went into the locker room and asked us where we wanted the camera pointing to next. We told them that we didn't care, just to use their judgment and place the video camera where they thought best. They decided to point the camera into the storage room. There it stayed until the end of the investigation.

After reviewing the video at home, there were a few things that we captured on video that night in the old locker room. When the video camera was facing the faucet / sink area, we did get a white wisp of smoke that started near the upper right corner and moved across to the left side of the camera. There was also a possible EVP. I say possible because we can't be 100% sure due to the fact that members were coming and going into the room during the investigation. So we can't be totally sure that what we recorded was them or a spirit. There were also a few strange and unaccountable noises that the video camera picked up, but the noises were not in view of the camera. Again though, we can't be sure who made the noises.

The activity had slowed down to almost nothing after a sustained flurry of activity that had lasted an hour or so. We decided to call it a night and pack it in. It took us over 30 minutes to unhook, collect, and pack up all of the equipment that we had brought with us. We only had a few minutes to spare before Jim came to lock up so we had timed it just about right.

Conclusion – We feel that this school has activity. We can't be sure though if the activity is caused by past students or by the property itself. By this I mean that the spirits may not be attached to the school but they are attached to the land. The land was here way before the school has been standing in this spot. And if there were any kind of tragic, emotional events, this might have caused a spirit or two to stick around and call this school home.

A Tragic Event...

Date: 04-28-07
Location: St. Clair Shores

When the family contacted us they were already at wit's end. They were having major problems and the family was seriously having concerns about staying in their own house.

They were at a point where they feared for their safety in their home. Some of the things that were happening were very threatening in nature. They contacted us to do an investigation, determine what was there, and rid the home of the spirits if possible.

We broke tradition and ate at Wendy's before the investigation. I say we broke tradition because we usually eat at McDonald's. We always joke and say that one day McDonald's will sponsor us. We playfully say things like "SEMGHS always eats at McDonald's before we investigate homes" or "McDonald's, the official fast food restaurant of SEMGHS," we have fun with this. And like we are fond of saying, "Never say never."

We all had a hearty meal and headed off to the house. The house was a nice house, 2 stories, and a good sized backyard. We were met by the family at the door and we went in. We said our hellos and asked the family if they had any questions about the investigation. They had no questions so the team went out to our vehicles and brought in the equipment.

We commandeered the living room and set up the equipment there. We had 3 video monitors, a laptop, VCR, temperature probe, and a motion sensor. When we do an investigation in a home, we literally take over the house. We have equipment, cables, and of course of members.

We take this time before the tour of the house that the owners give us to unpack the equipment and put batteries in everything that need them. We also have some equipment that are temperature sensitive so we need to acclimate these to allow them to get an accurate temperature, this is especially important when we do investigations in the winter.

When everything was unpacked, batteries installed, cameras ready, we had the family give us the tour of the house. We ask them that they don't give out too much information about the activity. They can tell us things like what sort of activity happens here, what is felt there. We ask that they don't give specifics like Uncle Don died here on the couch, or Mr. Smith was the previous owner and he died in the kitchen. The reason for this is pretty simple. We have some members that are mediums. They can sense things like names, how the spirit passed, what the spirits look like, etc. When we are told information before hand and then during the investigation we start getting things we don't know if what we are getting was from the homeowner telling us or we got them on our own. We just like to eliminate all possible outside sources of information.

We started the tour in the average sized living room. If you continued out of the living room, you came to a small hall. To your left at the end of the hall were 2 bedrooms, one on each side of the hall. There was a closet that was shared by both rooms, so you could look through the closet and see into the other bedroom or you could walk through the closet from one bedroom to the other bedroom. To your right, through a short hallway was the kitchen. If you walked through the kitchen you would come to a Y in the hallway. To your left and after a short walk was the master bedroom. If you went right you went up the stairs to the second floor. Once upstairs you would walk through a small room then up 2 stairs. Straight ahead in the corner was the computer and to your left was another hallway. Immediately off the hall on your left, near the computer was a bedroom. Continue straight and the hallway ends at another bedroom. If you came back down the stairs, at the bottom and on your left was a door to the outside. In the backyard were 2 sheds. We found out later during the investigation that there used to be an in ground pool that was filled in years ago.

The house was pleasant enough. Nicely decorated and had a homey feeling about it. There was no indication that anything was wrong with this house. But as we have found out over the years houses can be deceiving.

During our walkthrough the family showed us the house and the rooms where there had been activity, she told us what had happened in rooms that have had activity. During this time we identified 3 potential hot spots.

The first one was in the downstairs bedroom at the end of the hall. There had been reports of an apparition of an older woman in this room. While we were doing our walkthrough I was in the bedroom on the right and was near the closet. As I looked into the closet I saw a reflection of a woman in the mirror in the other bedroom. If you remember from the beginning of this investigation I mentioned that the closet was accessible from both bedrooms. I asked who was in the other bedroom, I received no answer. I quickly went through the closet into the other bedroom and there was no one there. I went back through the closet to the original bedroom, the one on the right, and there is when I encountered a "talker." There was a spirit that wanted to talk. I can see things and sense things that not everyone can. The one thing I can't do is hear voices when spirits are talking to me. What I hear is a buzzing sound in my ear. When I get this sensation I know that a spirit is trying to talk to me. When this happens I tell the spirit to show me what they are trying to tell me because I can't hear them. I ask them to put an image in my mind of what they are trying to tell me. When I asked this of the spirit the buzzing sensation stopped. Either the spirit moved to a different spot in the house or it became frustrated with me for my lack of comprehension of what it was trying to tell me and just stopped talking to me. We would make contact again later that night. The woman I had seen was an older woman with grey hair that was in a bun. There was no one in the house at that moment that matched that description. I told the family what I had seen and she said that her daughters have seen the same woman in that room. We set up a video camera on a tripod facing the closet. We also put a motion detector in the room facing the closet. Even after the promising start in this room, with the grayed hair woman, we didn't get anything on video in here the whole investigation.

The second area where we decided to setup equipment was the master bedroom. During the walkthrough we were picking up some EMF spikes here. It was also here that behind closed doors it was reported that heavy workout equipment was turned over. Charles put one of his camera's here along with a motion detector. This room we actually closed off to traffic to better increase our chances of getting something. Charles got a few orbs on video from this room.

Finally we put another video camera, motion detector, and Trifield EMF in the upstairs by the computer. The homeowners have reported that while sitting in the chair by the computer that you would feel like either you were being watched or the feeling that someone was standing behind you looking over your shoulder. When they would turn around, no one was there. During the investigation numerous orbs were seen on video and by using the monitor downstairs we were able to see them in real time, moving near and close to the computer.

With the moderate success of the video camera's getting the orbs on tape and the EMF spikes we were getting throughout the house, this investigation could be considered a success. However it was the events leading up to the very last minute of the investigation that would set this investigation apart from the rest and even possibly the greatest satisfaction, on a personal level, that we have had so far as a ghost hunting organization.

All during the investigation we were getting high EMF readings throughout the house. This is actually odd because usually you will get EMF readings in parts of the house but not the whole house. In past investigations we might have a bad outlet or a fuse box on the outside wall. In those cases you will have an EMF spike in that area, not in the WHOLE house. If you get EMF readings all over the place this sometimes could be attributed to bad wires which in turn could cause electricity to leak into the house.

No matter where we went, the living room, kitchen, bedrooms, or the hallway the whole house was giving off EMF readings. We had some members go out into the backyard. They called me on the radio to come out back. I met up with them outside and they wanted me to see that they were getting EMF readings in the BACKYARD also. The main area was just past the filled in pool to the farthest shed. This isn't totally uncommon as some towns have underground power lines which will give off EMF readings. However, these spikes were moving. They would be by the pool one minute then the spike would be gone. We would walk around the yard and we would get another spike by the shed. Then that would stop and then another one would pop up near the fence at the back on the yard. The spikes were moving around the whole yard, not staying in the same place for more than a few minutes. Underground power lines would not give off EMF readings like this. With underground power lines, you will get EMF spikes in one and only one area and these will stay constant. Overhead power lines will not fluctuate as they will give you a constant EMF reading.

At one point we did get one spot that had a constant reading for a few minutes. The area was 3-4 feet in diameter and no more than 5 feet high and was between the filled in pool and the fence at the end of the property. We got constant readings in this area; there were no spikes just a constantly high reading. Holly took a picture during the time we had a high EMF spike and she got what looks like a little boy in yellow trunks standing past the group near the fence.

During the time outside we were getting some "visions" of things that had happened in the past. One member, Jeff, kept on seeing what he referred to as a pool party. He saw the pool, before it was filled in, food set up on tables and people standing around talking. The time that this party took place would have been either the late 50's or early 60's.

I myself saw the same thing, not the exact thing as far as the details were concerned, but the same idea as a pool party with food and conversation. But I also saw something else. The time flashed ahead to the present to when the pool had been filled in.

You have to ask yourself why an in-ground pool would be filled in. Sure it is a hassle with the maintenance and chemicals, but when you have one put in it would be safe to say that you know what is involved with having a pool.

Let me explain the meaning of something that I will probably refer to at some point in this book. I might refer to something called "my minds eye." This isn't really an eye in my mind. It is but isn't. The mind's eye is the ability to tap into events that have happened both in the past and future. So when someone says that he saw an apparition in his mind's eye, anyone else would not have seen the apparition.

What I saw in my mind's eye was the pool. I "saw" tiny wet footprints coming out of the pool and walking around the edge away from me. I didn't see where they went but maybe the person leaving them was involved in the party we saw from years ago and was heading for maybe a bite to eat at one the tables we saw around the pool. This is a great example of seeing something in my minds eye. There is no pool now, there is no concrete visible, but I SAW the wet footprints come out of the pool and walk around it. There was no remote possibility that anyone could have seen this since the pool is filled in now. What I saw in my mind's eye happened years ago.

When I saw the footsteps coming from the pool I got this very intense feeling of anger. The feeling was one of uncontrollable anger and sorrow. The sensation was coming from the corner of the pool, where the master bedroom is now. I asked the owner if the bedroom was original to the house or built on. I was told that the bedroom was original but wasn't always a bedroom. It was a pool changing room before being converted to a bedroom. That might explain the weight equipment being tipped over. I was getting a feeling of intense anger and somehow the weight equipment was a part of that.

The feeling that members of the group and I were getting was that the pool was somehow an important part of the activity the family was experiencing. We were at an early part of the investigation so we didn't know exactly how it played out in all of this.

We continued the investigation outside. We were still getting regular EMF spikes all over the backyard. The EMF readings we were getting are consistent with readings that are generally regarded as paranormal in nature. That range being 2.0 – 8.0. I stayed outside for a few more minutes then went back inside to see how the investigation was progressing. A few members stayed outside to monitor the EMF readings that were continuing.

At this point in the investigation we had 3-4 members in the yard, 2 in the living room, and 3 upstairs with the homeowner. Adam was one of the members upstairs. The homeowners told us that when they would be sitting at the computers upstairs they would often feel like they were being watched or they would feel a cold spot near the computer. Once the homeowner was on the computer talking with a relative, they have web cameras set up to do this. The person she was talking to asked her who was standing behind her. The family looked behind her and no one was there. The person told her that on their computer screen they saw a man clearly and that he was standing right behind her. Again she looked behind the chair and she could see no one.

Adam had this good idea of having the homeowner sit at the computer and see if we can get whoever would stand behind her to make an appearance for us. To anticipate this we set up a motion detector in the hall upstairs along with the Trifield EMF and a video camera. The Trifield EMF and video camera were pointed directly at the computer. If anything was to show themselves to us we would get it on video.

I was still downstairs when Adam called me on the radio and asked that I came upstairs. They were getting cold breezes by the computer and the EMF meters were going off the scale. I told him I would be up there is in a few minutes.

When I reached the upstairs the family was sitting at the computer. Adam was to her right, slightly behind, in a chair. One of the daughters was on the couch and the other was sitting in the hall near the computer desk. The EMF meter that Adam was holding was registering some kind of EMF spike as the lights and beeping sound were all going off. Adam said the EMF meter started to spike right after the homeowner sat at the computer then said that she felt someone was looking over her shoulder, but it wasn't Adam. In fact, Adam was 5 feet from her sitting on a chair in the corner. He was nowhere near her.

I sat down next to the small desktop fridge they had upstairs. I was no more than 20 feet from the computer desk with both Adam and the homeowner in plain sight. I tried to get a handle on who might be there with us, spirit wise that is. I immediately sensed that there were 4 spirits in the room with us. One was by herself, not attached to the other spirits. She was the more passive spirit. Two of the spirits were little boys. The fourth and last spirit was that of a man, he told me that his name was Tom. He was the angry spirit we picked up in the master bedroom. He was not very nice.

The female spirit told me her name was Beatrice. But she said I could call her "Bea." I couldn't get a time period for her but she had on a full length dress with an apron over it. She had grey hair and wore it in a bun. Then it dawned on me that Bea was the woman I saw in the bedroom downstairs. I asked her if it was indeed her that I had seen downstairs and she said yes. She told me that other members of the family had also seen her and that she didn't mind them being in her house. That struck me as being funny. She didn't mind them being in HER house. This lovely woman had died years ago and she still thought of the house as hers.

The 2 boys that were also in the house wouldn't tell me their names. They must have been taught never to give their names to strangers and they were still doing what they were told in death. I didn't get too much from them. To help the story flow easier I will refer to the oldest as Dean and the youngest as Sam. When they would talk to me, it would be in direct response to my questions. They never offered any more than what was asked and were not very talkative to me. I did feel that they were brothers, one had on yellow bathing trunks; remember the picture Holly had taken outside. This would be later confirmed by the family as they had seen the little boy in the house before.

Tom was very demanding and a no nonsense type of spirit. The homeowner had asked us to clean the house and help the spirits cross over. Tom made it very clear, in no uncertain terms, that he would not leave and that we couldn't make him leave. We have encountered spirits like this before and with some persuasion have helped them cross over. But this case I thought would be a lot harder than previous ones. The spirit was very steadfast in his stance that he would not leave the house.

The investigation at this point was only 2 hours into the 4 hours that we normally take to conduct an investigation. The give and take with the spirits lasted another two more hours. It would be impossible to accurately write the whole transcript what was said to what spirit and what the spirits said to us, and give it any justice. I will condense the last two hours into the most poignant part of the interaction between us and the spirits.

Piecing together the things we were getting from the Sam and Dean and Tom's spirits, adding in some lucky guesses we were able to determine that the boys and man spirit were related. Tom was Sam and Dean's father. We were dealing with a family, minus the mother. We needed to figure out then what had happened to them and why the three remained in the house. This task was harder than we could ever have imagined.

We had asked the Tom to cross over. We told him that there were people he knew and loved waiting for him on the other side. He was very steadfast that he would not cross over. While we were trying to persuade him to cross over, both of the boy spirits came into the room. They were in the same room as their father but they couldn't see him in the room with them. At one point we told the boys that their father was in the same room as they were. Dean told me that they couldn't see their father but that they wanted us to tell his father that he was sorry. Sorry for what we wondered? Dean wouldn't go into detail but kept repeating it over and over, "I am sorry dad."

We were getting very frustrated because we couldn't determine the reason for this scene that was playing out in front of us. No two investigations are the same but we usually have little or no problem figuring out the cause of a haunting and helping the spirits involved crossover. But in this case, we were getting nowhere with the spirits involved.

The whole time we were talking with Tom and the spirits of his two boys, Bea was just standing in the shadows, content with just watching the whole scenario play out. It was as if she had seen the spirits for all these years and she herself wanted closure for the father and his boys.

Sometime during my communication with the spirits, one of our members, Bryan came over and sat a few feet from me, on my right. I didn't see him sit down but that is not too uncommon when I am talking to the spirits. This is because when I talk to the spirits I do so with my eyes closed as this helps me to concentrate and I usually zone out entirely when doing this and I don't have any awareness of things that are happening around me.

I had asked the Tom one more time to crossover and Bryan said "No, I will not." To say that what he said totally shocked me would be an understatement. I am not usually at a loss for words but in this instance I was. I just looked over to him I am sure with a puzzled look on my face. I think I said something like "What did you say?" Bryan looked at me and said he didn't know where that came from. He said the words but they were not his. It was almost like someone put that thought in his head.

What Bryan did was channel. When someone channels, they open themselves up so the spirit can take over his/her body and communicate through him or her. I have does this many times. You have to be careful and be grounded so the spirit doesn't totally take you over. This would be bad.

The next few minutes I would ask Tom to cross over and Bryan would answer me. He wasn't answering me though; Tom was talking through Bryan, using Bryan's voice to be heard.

Here is a little of the give and take that went on:

Me: I told the male spirit to cross over. There will be friends and relatives waiting there to see you.

Tom (Through Bryan): "I don't believe you."
Me: "Why don't you believe me?"
Tom: "You are lying to me"
Me: "Why would I lie to you?"
Tom: "Don't trust you"
Me: "I have no reason to lie to you. We are here to help you."
Tom: "I still don't trust you"
Me: "Why"
Tom: "Because"

As you can see from our conversion we were getting absolutely no where with Tom. We were running out of ideas to help the Tom cross over. No matter what we said to him he wasn't going to leave. We needed to figure out what was keeping him here.

Then it dawned on me. Sometimes something will be right in front of me in clear sight and it takes awhile to figure it out. This was one of those times. I knew what was keeping the male spirit here. The boys were. Earlier in the night I kept hearing "I am sorry dad." This was repeated over and over but I couldn't get anymore from the boys.

So if the boys were indeed keeping the male spirit here, all would we need to do was get them together and cross them over all at the same time. For some reason they were in the same house but couldn't see each other. They were looking for him and Tom was looking for Sam and Dean and they just were not meeting up with each other. Another thing we needed to figure out, why they weren't seeing each other. This was turning out to be a massive undertaking to cross these spirits over.

We decided to take another approach. Even though the boy spirits were not talking to us, if we could somehow gain their trust and get them to be open with us we might know then what tragic event is holding the family here. So we tried to open up a dialog with the boys.

All this time that we were communicating with their dad Sam and

Dean seemed to be hiding in the shadows. If we were on a Hollywood soundstage it would be the equivalent of being just off camera. They seemed perfectly willing to let the dad talk to us. We needed to change that.

We started by telling the boys that we were talking with their dad. Which was true, we were. We then told them that their dad was not mad at them anymore. Which wasn't entirely true but we were taking liberty that the dad wasn't mad anymore.

I told the boys that I heard them say "We are sorry dad." I then asked them, "What are you sorry about"? No response. I told them that I wouldn't be mad at them for what they did, I just wanted to help them because I didn't know what happened. This must have opened the floodgates because Dean started talking like a chatterbox. It was if he was relieved that he could get this off his chest.

Dean told us that there was a pool party in the backyard, which we had "seen" and that his father told him to watch his younger brother Sam while the father went inside the house. The father was only going to be gone for a few minutes. After the father had left Dean made sure to keep an eye on his younger brother. Dean turned his back only for a few seconds and when he turned back his brother was gone. He was frantic with worry, where could he be? The father came back and asked Dean where his brother was. He told his father "I don't know. I only turned my back for a moment." Now the father was worried and angry. Why didn't he watch his younger brother like he was asked to?

They searched frantically. They searched all around the pool, the whole yard, and even went into the house. Hoping against hope that Sam had slipped inside without his father seeing him. Nothing, it was like the child had vanished.

Then they heard a scream from the pool. Tom and Dean ran out to the pool. They were horrified at what they saw. One of the guests had dove into the pool and was holding Sam. Somehow he had slipped into the pool and ended up in the deep end. No one saw that he was at the bottom of the pool. They didn't think to look there. The father grabbed Sam's lifeless body from the arms of the guest and gently sat him down by the waters edge. They tried and tried to bring him back to life but he was already gone.

The father was stricken with grief. He let out an unworldly scream and sobbed uncontrollably. Dean, whom the father had put in charge of watching his younger brother, started to cry quietly. It was an accident. He only turned away for a few seconds. At this point he wished that he was dead also.

The father went into an angry rage. He was throwing around the furniture near the pool. He went into the changing room and started to throw the furniture around in there also. He had no control of what he was doing. His whole reason for living was gone. He still had a son left but he hated him at that moment. Dean had let him down by not watching Sam like he had asked of him.

For the rest of their lives the father never forgave Dean for the drowning. He knew deep inside that it was an accident, but the pain was just too great.

They had spent all the years trying to find each other in the spirit world after the Tom and Dean passed on. None of the three spirits, the father and his two sons, had crossed over. Now that we knew what happened, crossing them over just got a lot easier.

I looked and Bryan was still sitting next to me. I was hoping the father was still able to talk through Bryan. I told the father that his sons were by the pool waiting for him and that he needed to go to them now. The father, still talking through Bryan, still didn't believe me and said that he still would not leave. I told the father that if he went to the pool and his kids weren't there he was more than welcome to come back and we would continue to talk. But I told him he wouldn't be coming back because they indeed were there waiting for him.

Bryan said that he felt the father leave the room and thought he was going to the pool. I faintly heard a beeping sound and realized that Adam still had his EMF meter on and that it was still getting high EMF spikes. I concentrated on the boys and I told the people in the room that the father was there with his sons. They were hugging each other and crying. All three were telling each other that they were sorry and all was forgiven.

While I was in contact with them I reminded them that they were all together again, a family, and that they needed to cross over. Then I got the feeling that they were gone. And at that very moment I said they were gone, Adam's EMF stopped. Just like that, there were no more EMF readings.

The room was totally quiet. No one said a word. It was a combination I think of being in awe of what happened and realizing that a boy had drowned in the pool and that was the cause of the hauntings.

After everyone composed themselves in the room, Adam, Paul, and Jeff went outside and through the house taking EMF readings. There was nothing. Absolutely nothing was being picked up by the meters. There was not one stray EMF reading in the whole house or the yard. Where we had previous EMF spikes during the investigation there was nothing now. It was like all the activity and EMF readings were caused by the father and his two sons. It was a draining experience and was well worth it. We helped the father and his 2 sons to not only crossover but we gave the homeowners piece of mind.

What about Bea you asked? She was still in the house. She didn't want to cross over and she was perfectly happy where she was. We don't usually like to keep spirits here on this plane of existence, as we prefer that they cross over so they can continue their journey. In this case we decided to let Bea stay. She was happy in the house and the homeowners had no problems with her being there.

With our work seemingly finished we decided this would be a good time to call it an evening. We gathered our equipment, packed it up and packed it in the van. We didn't see the need to clean the house because we believed that the cause of the hauntings had crossed over to the other side.

To reassure the homeowners I told them that I would walk through the house and yard to see if I felt anything and to see if anything was left behind. I didn't feel any spirits were left in the house, except Bea. We said our good-byes and went home.

Conclusion: The activity was most definitely linked to the father trying to find his two sons and also to the tragic drowning that happened years ago in the backyard. The overturned weight equipment in the master bedroom we think was the father showing his anger and frustration to the events of losing his son. We haven't heard anything from the family since the investigation. This is usually a good sign. To the best of our knowledge the activity has not returned to the house.

Work Is Never Finished...

Date: 1998
Location: Somewhere in Michigan

Although we have never conducted an investigation in this building, there are some stories to tell about this location. The building was as far as we know a elementary school, a catholic school, and currently is a bank building. Brenda and I used to work there in the late 1990's. We had some strange things happen to us and stories that we heard from co-workers and friends of their experiences in the building. Here are some of those stories.

In this chapter however I will not be going into great detail on the layout of the building. The reason for this is simple. The building is huge. There are so many hallways, rooms, and stairs that it would take many pages to accurately give the details of the building. There are two stories from our friend Kirby. The first happened in a small office near the computer room. The bank has these automatic doors that when they sense movement they will open. When they open the doors will slide to one side. Very much like the doors on the USS Enterprise on TV's "Star Trek." This particular room had two sets of doors. One that opened into the room and the other door opened into the hallway. Kirby was sitting at a desk when the door closest to him suddenly slid open. Then as if someone was walking out of the room the door that led into the hallway opened also. Then both doors slid close. These doors open only on movement. Someone or something would have had to go in front of the sensor to open the door like that. Kirby said that he was sitting at the desk the whole time that the doors opened and closed by themselves. No one left the room that he could see and he wasn't close enough to the doors to trip the sensors, thus making them open. He never learned what caused the doors to open and close the way they did that day. As far as he knows there is no explanation for this, other than maybe the spirits had finished with their business in the room and left.

Another story from Kirby happened in a different room in the building. Kirby said that he walked into a room and turned a corner to get to his desk. When he turned the corner there was a man sitting at his desk. The man was middle aged with thinning hair, a brown three piece suit, and either writing something or making notes on a piece paper. The man at the desk looked up and was as startled to see Kirby as Kirby was to see him. They stared at each other for a few seconds and then Kirby said the man just slowly dissolved away until he was no longer sitting at the desk. Literally the man was there one minute, gone the next. Kirby has seen the man since then. Usually he is sitting at a desk, working on something that he will never complete.

This comes from one of Brenda's friends at the bank. When you come in the employee entrance, past the guard shack, you will find a long hallway. The hallway goes from just past the guard shack to the front of the building, then you make a left and you will go past the executive offices in the front of the building and you can take the hallway to the left and it will take you back towards the back of the building or continue straight and that leads you to the front door. If you start at the guard shack the entrance to the printer room and computer room, both on your left, and telephone banking in on your right. Telephone banking has two doors in which to enter. You can see everything in this hallway from the back of the building to the front. There is no hiding in this hallway. Brenda's friend, whose name was Jim, who worked in the computer room told us that one time at work, he worked midnights, he was walking towards the back of the building to delivery some work to someone that would be in early in the morning. He was just going to put the work on the person's desk and head back to the computer room. This was around 5-6 AM and there weren't too many people in the building. Telephone banking was closed as nobody would be showing up for work for a few hours. Jim had dropped off the work and was heading back to the computer room. Again, he had a clear view of the hall all the way to the front of the building. As Jim was walking down the hall he saw a woman, dressed in jeans and a white top, wearing sneakers with blonde hair walk into telephone banking. The woman that he saw came down the hall from the front of the building. Jim saw the woman for a split second, just the amount of time needed to come into view in the hallway and into telephone banking. Jim knew that no one should be in the building at this hour, and certainly not in telephone banking. Jim went into the first door for telephone banking, which was closest to him and the farthest door from which the woman had entered. Once you enter the room you are standing in one big room. There are cubicles for each person but no walls. You can clearly see from one end of the room to the other. No one was there. The woman Jim had seen enter the room was nowhere to be seen. Jim went through the whole room and couldn't find the woman. The woman had entered the far door and was out of view for only a few seconds before our friend entered the other door. If the woman had entered the room and then left quickly Jim would have seen the woman. After not being able to find her in telephone banking, Jim did a search of the building and there was no sign of the woman. To this day Jim will swear up and down that he saw this woman but has no idea who she was or where she went. He didn't see the woman again on his shift.

Let me tell you how the whole "we have a ghost thing" got started. As you may expect this is not something you talk about in normal conversations. Unless of course you are ghost hunters. Then if you are like us we plan some of our vacations to places that are supposedly haunted. I started working midnights in the print room. There were just two of us in there, Karen and myself. When I was in there the conversation never touched on the whole ghost thing. I was in the print room for just under a year. Then I was promoted to computer operator I and literally moved through the sliding glass doors to the next room. Well, one slow night I was on the internet searching for ghost groups. I happened to stumble on the one I am in charge of now. Back then I was just a member of this group. To keep a long story short I left the computer screen up on a ghost picture page. One of my co-workers happened by my screen and saw the pictures. She then asked me "You know that there are ghosts in the building right?" Okay, here we go again. We know you are interested in ghosts so let's mess with the guy thing. So I went along with it. She told me to ask Karen about it. She will tell you the same thing. Things have happened to Karen while in the building.

I can go along with a good joke, even if it's on me, so I walked into the next room and asked Karen about the ghosts that were in the building. Totally expecting to look into the computer room and see my fellow co-workers rolling on the floor in uncontrollable laughter for the joke they just played on me. To my surprise Karen nodded her head and told me that yes, we do have ghosts in here. Then of course my interest peaked and she told me that she had only had two things happen to her in this building.

One thing that did happen to her was sometimes hearing her name being called and turning around and not finding anyone there. She said that it was a man's voice. It always sounded like it was coming from a few feet behind her.

Another time Karen, Starla, Jan, and myself were all in the printer room talking. Starla and Jan also worked with me in the computer room. Part of my job was to check on the networking computers to make sure they were up and running. I was on my way to do this when Starla and Jan came into the print room from the hallway. Karen was already in the room so we just started talking. I can't remember what we were talking about. I am sure that the conversation didn't last too long. I continued on to check on the computers and Starla and Jan went back to the computer room. I did my check on the computers and they were all working as they should so I was heading back to my desk. Karen stopped me and told me that after we had stopped talking and she was alone again in the room she heard a man call her name and it sounded like it was coming from right behind her. She turned around quickly but no one was there.

This would always happen in the print room. This room is where all the printing was done for the bank. We had two printers set up to print two sided jobs. This printer ran almost the whole length of the room. The room was longer width wise than length wise. Behind the main printers were four small pin feed printers. These printers were used for small jobs, usually checks and smaller reports. To the right (if you were facing the computer room) was the storage room. We stored the big, 800 lb rolls of paper for the main printer in here. They were 3 to a pallet, and we usually had anywhere between 5-6 pallets at one time there.

There were 3 doors to the print room. There was an automatic sliding door that was accessible from the hall towards the back of the room as well as an automatic sliding door that opened into the computer room. In the left corner was a door that went into networking.

There were occasions after I was transferred to the computer room that I would work in the print room. This would only happen if Karen was gone or it was really busy and she needed help. There were two of us in the print room until I was moved to the computer room then Karen was by herself since they didn't hire anyone to replace me.

That storage room would always bug me. I would swear that when I was sitting down at the desk I would always see movement in there out of the corner of my eye. If you were sitting at the desk sorting work the storage room would be all the way to your right. Maybe I was just being paranoid or just reacting subconsciously to the stories I was hearing, but I know there was something moving in there.

On one occasion, I myself heard my name being called. I was alone in the print room as Karen had called in sick. I sat at my desk sorting work and I distinctly and clearly heard my name being called. It was hard to tell where exactly it came from but if I had to guess it originated somewhere near the pin feed printers in the back of the room. I turned around and no one as there. I tried to pass it off as the printers, my own imagination, or maybe even a fellow co-worker playing a joke on me.

I got up from my chair and went back to pin feed printers. I just stood there for a few minutes to see if I could pinpoint where the sound came from. I didn't hear anything so I started back to the desk so I could sort more work. I walked no more than a few feet when I heard my name called again. This time the voice was right near my right ear, as if someone was standing right next to me and whispered in my ear. I spun around. I could safely say that it wasn't my co-workers messing with me. No one was there and if someone was there, they had no time what so ever to either hide or leave the room before I spun around and caught them red-handed. There went the co-worker theory.

I was pretty sure, not totally, but close to it that the printers were not making that noise. I heard my name being called and the last time it came from right behind me.

Another bit of information. There was a hallway that ran on the other side of the computer room that Brenda would avoid at all cost. She didn't like it. Nothing bad happened to Brenda in that hall. She just got this bad feeling whenever she walked the hallway. Brenda just stopped using the hallway and everything was okay in her eyes.

Conclusion: Is the building haunted? In my humble opinion, yes, it is haunted. There are too many stories from friends and co-workers. Things that happened to me cannot be explained. Granted, I didn't speak to every worker in the building. That would be almost impossible due to running three shifts a day. But I can imagine some of the stories they could tell. Especially from the people that were in the building alone during the second shift. I know on the midnight shift, the one I worked; there were some very interesting stories. I would like to do some research one day and find out who the girl and the older gentleman in the suit were. If they were still there in the building after they had passed there has to be a reason why. Is there a message they are trying to tell us and people are not listening? Do they just like the location so much that they don't want to leave? The bank was bought out a few years ago. I left to work for another company right after they announced the buyout. I know they closed most of the departments in that building but a few people still work there. I wonder if they have been introduced to the resident spirits that seem to wander the corridors.

Have to Start Somewhere...

Date: 09-21-00
Location: House in Pontiac.

I remember this house well, being that it was our "first" house investigation. This is what gave us our break and we haven't slowed down yet. We had just done a radio interview with a Detroit radio station. There was nothing spectacular about the interview just a few minutes of questions and answers. The radio station gave out our web address. A few days later we were contacted by the homeowner requesting an investigation. The funny thing is she wanted to have someone come over but didn't know where to look or whom to ask. Then she was driving in her car when the interview came on the radio. Call it what you will but we think there was some higher powers that came together on this one. We called the homeowners and had talked to them at length about their activity. We agreed on a time and date for their investigation.

We called her as we were on the road because we were going to be late. We had hit serious road construction, which is a passage of season from winter to spring, here in Michigan. She told us that she would take the mattress down that was in front of the door. Being our first home investigation and not knowing what to expect this comment made us more than a little nervous. Brenda prodded her for more information. The upstairs of the house was one big room, with the stairs leading down to the first floor. They had put the mattress in front of the door coming from upstairs to keep the spirits from coming down and scaring the children. Our minds were at ease now but what exactly were we getting ourselves into with this investigation?

That was the main reason she had asked us to come out, it was scaring her children. The children were seeing things that were scaring them. We have found that children and animals can see things that we can't.

The house was a nice house with an enclosed front porch. When you first walked into the house you were standing in the living room. Behind you to the left was the mom's bedroom. There was a bedroom to your upper left, and then a room that took you to the stairs that led up into the attic. The attic was actually big enough and finished to be a fairly good sized bedroom. Directly in front of you, if you are standing in the living room, was a dining area, then through the door way was the kitchen, and off to the left was a door that led downstairs into the basement.

We were so new at this investigation stuff as this was our first attempt at doing a home investigation that we didn't even meet at a restaurant. We actually met, if you can believe it, in a parking lot a few miles from the house. How bad was that? When I think of our first meeting place all I can do is shake my head in disbelief.

We had some equipment for this investigation but not much. We had a 35MM camera, but no digital one yet. This we would learn can actually dampen an investigation because you can't see the pictures immediately, so you don't know if you should continue taking pictures or not if you get a positive picture. I think that we just had a motion detector and I do remember this, a very inexpensive and easy to use EMF detector.

The activity was focusing on her eldest boy. She told us that once he was playing on the enclosed front porch. He came into the house covering his eyes and told his mother to make it go away. The boy told us that a man was with him on the front porch and wouldn't leave him alone. Any parent would react with the news with shock and anger. The mom asked where the man was and the boy said that the man was standing right behind him. She looked but there was no one there. Another time they were all sleeping in the mom's bed. Early in the morning the boy woke up screaming saying that he saw a man's torso from the waist up coming through the ceiling, upside down, and that the man was opening his mouth and screaming but no sound was heard. The spirit of this man got some sick satisfaction from terrifying this poor boy. In this case the personality of the man stayed with him after death, he was just mean towards children.

They also had a parakeet in a cage in the dining room. The bird had lost almost all of its feathers and they were lying on the bottom of the cage. This bird was so nervous that if you even started towards the cage it would start chirping and acting like it was afraid. Again, here is where an animal also was sensing something in the house.

We had the usual amount of orbs on film but not much else. We had a couple of EMF spikes upstairs but pretty normal through out the rest of the house. We registered one cold spot in the bedroom. The homeowner had a dog and during most of the investigation it paced the hallway in front of the master bedroom. At one point it started to whimper like it was afraid of something, the dog was like a lab mix and was a pretty big dog. I doubt that it was afraid of much. The homeowner said that the dog was normally a calm one and she took him outside and put him in the back yard. The most interesting event happened about half way through the investigation in the upstairs room. We had placed two video cameras up there, and we had two members up there watching them and the video output on the screen. We heard a yell, then a yell for us to come upstairs. This was before we purchased two way radios! They had seen a flashing white light start on the ceiling, then cross the room, and then just disappear. They played the video back for us so that we could see what they had seen. It was a very interesting video. When the light crossed the room it didn't just cross the room and was on the walls. This light came off the walls and entered the room, like it had dimension. There were only two windows in the room, one on each end of the room, which was oblong. Since we were on the second floor there was no chance that it could have been cars passing the house, not up that high.

We had worked with a medium while there and we came to an interesting conclusion. It seems that there was a spirit of a man that had overdosed in the basement years ago. For obvious reasons he did not know that he was dead. From what I was told he had a wife and a couple of children. The thing that underscores this whole process was that he wanted to know why his family had left him. He thought that he was still alive, and he was sure that his family had left him and moved out. What I was told, was that he had a big fight with his daughter before he passed. She accused him of caring more about his drugs than he did his family. Now he was sorry for it. Because of that argument, he thought they walked out on him. In reality, when the man died, the family didn't want to stay in the house anymore. I believe they still live in the area. To them, they were just moving on with their life, and to him, they had left him. It really is sad to think about it. We told him that he had passed away, and it is my understanding that he did cross over and the house had less activity than it did before.

Our first house investigation went well. We still had some bugs to work out, and we definitely needed to buy some more equipment, especially a digital camera. One thing that I do clearly remember, was trying to find all that I could on how to conduct an investigation. I didn't want to look like this was our first home, even though it was, and I wanted us to look like we knew what we were doing. I found some things but they didn't really apply to us.

Conclusion- We do believe that there was some sort of presence in the home. From the child being scared to the poor bird in the cage leads one to believe that there was something paranormal in the house. The dog also reacted strange during the investigation. This investigation led to our being profiled on the Discovery Channel's "A Haunting."

Is That You, Grandpa??

Date: 04-27-02
Location: House in Ypsilanti

This investigation sounded like it was going to be a good one right from the initial contact from the homeowners. Let me give you a briefing of some of the activity they were experiencing.

The family consisted of the parents, two daughters, and a son. We will call the parents Mike and Gloria in this investigation. They had noticed a change in the behavior of the son. He was being combative at home, causing problems at school and basically trying to pick a fight with anyone that he could. Gloria told us that her son was generally a nice kid but something had changed recently. The two daughters slept in the bedroom off the kitchen but they would not play in their room with the door closed. The son's room was off the living room. Mike also told us that something strange was happening in the son's room. All three of the kids would be in there playing with the door closed and when the parents would check up on them they said that "Grandpa" was in there with them and that they all were playing tug of war. Sounds like a nice grandpa to play with the kids, but the only problem was that the grandpa had passed years ago. We were asked to come out and see what we could find in the house. We set up a date and time and agreed to come out to the house and see what we could do to help them.

The investigation site was a trailer in a trailer park. When you entered the trailer you were standing in the living room. Directly to your right was the kitchen and just off of that to the right was the girl's bedroom. If you went to the left through the living room and did a quick left turn you would hit a hallway, to your left was the son's bedroom. If you continued down the hallway you would hit the master bedroom. Half way down the hallway was a door on your right that led outside and to your left was the bathroom.

Mike and Gloria did tell us a little about the history of the house before we came out to do the investigation. It seems that before they moved in a child had died in the house. They had heard the child drowned in the tub but that circumstances of it were in question. They had heard from their neighbors that they child had tragically drowned but some of their neighbors claimed that it was no accident. Gloria said that the mom who had lived there before them had a drug problem and didn't want the child anymore and the mom had killed him. Mike had gone down to the manager's office to get more information but the manager would not give out any details and actually refused to talk about it.

By this time we had accumulated a little more equipment so we had more to use on this investigation. We had taken our readings and we started to set up in the house. We set up a motions detector in the hall and a few EMF meters in the kid's bedrooms. I don't think we had our video cameras yet so we didn't catch anything on video. We were getting EMF readings in the master bedroom. They had a crib as the mother was expecting, set up in the corner of the master bedroom near the foot of the bed. Jeff, one of our investigators, was getting high EMF readings near the crib. At which point he saw the blanket move as if someone had grabbed the corner and pulled it back. He took pictures of the area but didn't get anything.

The only thing that happened to us while onsite was the door to the outside, the one off the hallway by the master bedroom, opened up twice on its own accord. The first time there was three of us heading down the hall into the bedroom. It just swung open slowly, no big deal. We thought that maybe the door wasn't closed all the way and somehow it just opened up. We closed the door and made sure it was locked. We didn't think much of it. About half way through our investigation the door opened again. This time Mike was with us and he saw it also. This time he slammed the door to make sure it was closed and as an added measure of security he dead bolt locked it. Needless to say the door didn't open again that night.

An interesting side note to this investigation. We believed that we had identified a portal in the master bedroom; it was right behind the door. Previous owners, we believe, had been involved in Black Magic and had put a "protective" spell over the portal. Patrick and Dan, mediums that were present said that they could see a something inhuman trying to come out of the portal over to this side. They said that it had red eyes, horns, and claws for hands. The spell was acting as a cork if you will. As long as the spell was in place the beast couldn't come into this world. At no time, should anyone remove the spell, as long as it remained in place they felt nothing would come through the portal. Something interesting was covering the portal, or at least where we thought one was at. There was a child's sketch of a pirate's skull and crossbones. Was this just a coincidence or did it have some other meaning? We were very interested in this and the funny thing was the parents didn't even know the picture was there. It was right behind the door and the door was almost never closed.

We started asking everyone in the family if they knew how the picture got there. Of course, they all denied it. That is, until it was the boys turn to be asked. We asked him about it and he kind of hewed and hawed about answering the question. Gloria told him that he wasn't in any trouble but we needed to know how the picture got there. At this point we were all in the master bedroom looking at the picture. Finally he confessed that a boy at school dressed up as a pirate on Halloween and he told the son to draw the picture and place it at home on the very spot that we thought a portal was at. The parents told him okay and he went back into the living room. We didn't know if he was telling the whole story so we asked them to burn the picture. We didn't get a good feeling about it.

This was the picture drawn by a school friend that was covering the portal and keeping the non-human spirit from entering the master bedroom.

The investigation was essentially over so we asked the family if they had any questions for us. Mike and Gloria asked us if we could rid the house of the spirits. We told them that we would try. Cleansing a house consists of using incense, prayer, and in some extreme cases, Holy Water. The idea of cleansing a house is to help the spirits to cross over and go into the light. After we went through the whole house saying prayers and using incense, we used the incense around each person in the family. Brenda said that when I went around the boy he had a look on his face like "You can't hurt me" and he said "That stinks" which if you have ever smelled the incense it actually smells pretty good. We then made the sign of the cross with Holy Water on each family member's forehead. We bid them good bye and went home. They had strict instructions to call us if anything else happened.

We did get a phone call from them about a week later. She said the first night was rough. They have siding on the side of the house and they said during the night it sounded like something was throwing stones at the house. The spirits kept calling Mike and Gloria's names, wanting them to open the front door and let them back in the trailer. Mike said they knew better and it stopped during the night. They also reported that the son was 100% better, and that his attitude turned completely. He was helping his mom around the house again, he wasn't hitting her as he did before, and he was helpful and kind to his family and friends again. Also, their daughters would play in their room with the door closed now which they wouldn't do before we came out. During the phone conversation we had in the days following our investigation they thanked us again for helping. We told them they were welcome and that we were glad that we could help them.

As a side note to this, after an investigation we have tons of audio, video, and pictures to go over. As I was going through the pictures, we download them to our computer at home and all we kept on getting picture after picture were orbs. I remember going through the pictures almost in a trance state just from seeing the same type of pictures when I saw one that made me sit up a little straighter in the chair. There in the master bedroom was a picture of the mom and a few of our members. I remember they were talking about the pirate picture. Right behind the mom was a boy. We don't remember seeing him when the picture was taken. Also, where he appears to be standing was a glass night stand and there was a clock and other stuff on it. There wasn't enough room for a boy to be standing on this night stand. This is the actual investigation picture. What do you think?

An actual investigation picture at one of our investigations. We believe that the boy under the arrow is not real and is a spirit. A boy about the same age died years earlier in the home.

Conclusion-Now I will not say that what we did with the Holy Water and prayer is what definitely helped the family. The power of suggestion works wonders. I guess the bottom line here is that the family felt better in the home, the son was acting better, and all was good. So that is the important thing. Was there a portal in the house? We believe so. I don't think that anything was coming through the portal anymore but there was one there. We do also believe something was in the house, and probably it was taking the form of the grandpa to trick the kids and probably gain their trust. Who knows what the motive was behind this. All in all, this was a good investigation. Always makes us feel good when we can help a nice family like this.

*Update-We received an e-mail in 2004 from the owners of this trailer saying that some of the activity had come back and that they wanted us to come back out and check the place over a second time. We told them that we had a busy schedule but we would fit them in as soon as we could. We promised to get back with them in a few months. They agreed to this arrangement. Well, we received another e-mail a month later letting us know that they had moved out of state and that they obviously didn't need us to come back to their home. They didn't mention if the activity had anything to do with the move. We wish them luck in their new home.

WWII Connection...

Date: 11-23-03
Location: A house in Yale

From my understanding the homeowners have a connection to a newspaper in that part of the state. I don't know if they own it or work for it. Either way they wanted us to investigate the house plus the investigation would be the subject of a Halloween story for the paper. Unfortunately they asked us too late and we couldn't get out to the house in time for Halloween. We get booked months in advance for Halloween stories and we take them on a first come, first served basis.

The house was a nice, big old house, built in the 1920's. Ruth was only the second owner of the house, besides the original owners, and many of the previous family members have died of old age in the house. Ruth is doing a fabulous job at restoring it to its pristine looks when it was first built. There are two ways of getting into the house. Either through the front door, which would put you into the living room, or through a door into the kitchen, this is the way we came in. Where we came in, we were standing right in the kitchen. If you continued that way you would hit the hallway leading upstairs. If you turned to the left and walked a few feet you were in the dining room. If you continued straight you were in the living room. At the far end of the living room was a fireplace and to the left was the front door that led to the porch. About half way to the fireplace, and to your right, you were in the hallway. There were three rooms on the left of the hall. The last room on the left side of the hall was the master bedroom. When you passed the opening to the kitchen immediately on your right was a spare bedroom which we were told some people would not sleep in there at night preferring to sleep on the couch instead. There were stairs leading up to the second floor, and these were right next to the spare bedroom. Ruth was still in the process of redoing the whole upstairs so we didn't spend much time up there.

Some of the activity Ruth was experiencing was; they have seen a figure walking down the hall, doors would open and close on their own accord, and items were being moved around. The dog, although not afraid, would sometimes react to something, and stare into space, as if watching something that no one else could see.

When we arrived at the house we were surprised to see that Ruth had a food table laid out for us. She had everything from snacks to drinks. Although it was not required that Ruth had food for us it was appreciated. We usually meet before hand to eat somewhere close by, in this case we had Mickie D's. But the food was good never the less.

After we arrived on site we followed our procedures for doing an investigation. After all the equipment was brought in, we let the temperature equipment get acclimated to the temperature of the house. During this time Ruth led us on a tour of the house. This solves two purposes. It allows us to see the house and the other one is to give us a good idea where we will be putting our equipment, depending on any feelings that we might be getting.

We were taken from room to room, floor to floor, until all the rooms and knooks and crannies had been seen. It had the craftsmanship of bygone days when people took pride in their homes and houses were built to last. None of the rooms really stood out from the others and all the rooms felt pleasant enough.

There was a room, a spare bedroom off of the kitchen, that we had an interesting experience. When we first walked into the room

Brenda said that she felt like something happened in here that was extremely sad and Brenda said that there was a lot of emotion in the room. It was almost like you could feel a person crying in the room. Jeff, one of our members, in the mean time mentioned that he felt like it was something related to a War. Like someone went off to war and didn't return. Well, that would explain the feeling of great sorrow, and if that was the end of this story it would have made a good one. But hold on, there is more, and it gets better. We prefer that the owners not tell us any names that might be associated with the house. Not to be snobs or anything but we don't want to taint an investigation. Let me explain. We have some members that are mediums or sensitives. If the homeowner tells us that "Bob" dies in the house, and that "Grandma Millie" passed here, that might plant the names in our minds. Let's say that during the investigation we get the names of Millie and Bob. Did we get the information from the great beyond or did we remember the names from when the homeowners told us. Back to the room off of the kitchen. Jeff mentioned that he thought the feeling was associated from a war. When he said this Ruth turned white as a ghost, no pun intended, and I swear she was about to faint. Ruth told us to wait a minute that she needed to get something from the closet. What she brought back really blew our minds. Ruth had been shopping at an antique store and bought a lovely wedding dress. The dress was white and you could tell it was old. In the pocket of this garment was a letter. It wasn't really a pocket per se, but more like a little hidden area to put a few small things. The letter was written from a sailor in WWII to a girl back home. The letter talks about them and the uncertainly of what the future held during and after the war. If I remember correctly the letter was written in 1943. It is possible that the feelings we were getting were associated with the dress and letters, not actual people that lived in the house?

Another peculiar thing happened to us during the investigation. Ruth said that she has seen a figure walking down the hall. So we set up one of the wireless cameras on a wooden chair in the living room looking down the hallway facing the direction of the master bedroom. The chair never moved during the entire investigation. We were in the master bedroom, which is at the end of the hall on the left. We were trying to get EVP in the room. After about 15 minutes we exited the room. I was the first one out of the room. I took a step into the hall and watched as the camera that was placed on the wooden chair at the end of the hall fall on its side. No one was within 20 feet of it, the camera just toppled over. In hindsight it seemed like the camera fell in slow motion. Whether or not the camera fell on its own is up for debate. Perhaps the footsteps of us moving around during the two hour investigation could have caused enough vibration to cause the camera to fall over. The chair had no cushion and the camera was sitting directly on the wood. The true cause of the camera falling off the chair may never be fully known. When we started to watch the tape, due to technical difficulties, the camera was hooked up to the VCR wrong, and all that taped was a black picture for the whole investigation.

Conclusion- We had the usual orb pictures but little else. We didn't get anything on video, after discovering the mishap with the camera and VCR. It was a quiet night except for the camera falling off the chair during the investigation. However, just because nothing happened doesn't mean there wasn't anything there. For whatever reason the spirits were not active that night and didn't care to have their pictures taken, or want to make themselves known to us.

Helping a Lost Soul...

Date: 08-18-01
Location: A house in Troy

They say that timing is everything. We did an investigation during the annual "Dream Cruise" down Woodward Ave. in Detroit and spreading out to the suburbs. While the old cars that we saw on I-75 were great, the traffic was not. Once we got off the freeway things were better.

The house itself was a typical suburban home in Middle America. Tree lined, lawns neatly kept, and children's toys strewn about. Nothing would set this house apart from any in the area. The only thing that did was the type of activity the homeowner was experiencing.

The house was built in the 1940's. As far as we could determine there were no tragic events that had happened on the property. Joe, the owner of the house, has used the Ouija Board, but nothing else.

We came into the house via the front door, which put you smack dab in the living room. To your left was a short hallway that had a bathroom on your left, and then came to a dead end with bedrooms on both sides. From the living room you go straight and a little to your right and you are in the dining room. To your left was the kitchen and to your right was a side door that took you outside to the backyard.

The activity wasn't too bad. But again you can't chart this kind of thing and say this house had this or this house had that. People react to things differently and what might freak you out might be okay to another person. Joe had doors that would open on their own and cabinets that would do the same thing. Every now and then he would smell the scent of roses, even though there were no roses in the house at the time. The cable box would turn on, but you might be saying to yourself that it either had a bad battery or someone else with the same remote frequency near by was turning it on and off and this is feasible. Joe had the sensation of being pulled out of bed and his dog would sometimes act crazy like the dog could sense or maybe even see something that his master couldn't.

After the customary walk through with the owner we started to set things up. We had decided to use a monitor with the camcorder so we all could watch and see what happened during the investigation. One word of advice here, if you are trying something new, which we did by trying to use a monitor with the video camera, make sure everything works before you get to the site. For the life of me I couldn't get the dang monitor to work, all I kept on getting was a blue screen. Not only did I look like a fool but I was wasting valuable time messing with the thing. I finally got it figured it out. I had the connections from the camera to the monitor wrong. I had the input going to the output, took me awhile to figure this one out.

We had only one thing happen inside the house that was very interesting. We got two pictures; both digital that looked to us like half a person's body and the side of its head but it was always on the left side of the picture. You couldn't see any features because it was all white. At first we thought it was the proverbial finger in front of the flash. But these pictures were all white and in most cases if the finger is in the way, you will get a red to flesh color, usually not white. We couldn't rule out the finger completely, but we had enough confidence at the time to do so. One of the pictures was taken in the kitchen and the other one was outside. It was almost like something was trying to get our attention, which it did, without actually showing itself to us.

79

Towards the end of the investigation we migrated out back to see what was there. This is where Linda, one of our mediums started talking to, and conversing with the spirit that was there. If you don't believe in mediums or are skeptical about them, you might want to skip the next part. I was there, and I even had a hard time believing what I was hearing

Here is the story, as told to Linda by the spirit. The spirit that was causing the activity was an older gentleman, a farmer in his 70's. He owned the land when the area around Troy was mostly farmland. He told Linda that he was out farming the fields and he had sat down to eat the lunch that his wife had made for him. He sat down next to a big old tree for the shade. Unknown to him, there was a rattlesnake nest near the tree. The snakes must have felt threatened by this man because he said that they attacked him and bit him numerous times. The tree was quite a ways from the house so he knew that help would not get to him in time. He did pass from the bites. In this case he knew that he had passed, but he had absolutely no idea where to go. At this point Brenda took a picture of the back yard, it was perfectly clear. Linda then asked him if he saw a light. He would have to go into the light to cross over. He said that he did see the light and Linda told him that he would see people that he knew, and that they came for him and would help him cross over. He said that he did see people that he knew and that there were many of them. When he said this, Brenda took another picture. In a picture that a few minutes ago were clear, we now had a faint light on the left of the picture and orbs directly to the right of it. This is the "Light" that people say they see when they have near death experiences. Linda then told us that he had crossed over we immediately took another picture, and again, like the first one taken was perfectly clear. Wow, if you were there in the backyard you could have heard a pin drop. We were all in awe of the experience that we had just been through.

This is light on the left is often seen by people that have passed and have brought back to life. Linda was trying to cross over a spirit when this picture was taken.

At the time we didn't grasp what had just happened. We finished the investigation and nothing more was said of it. When the investigation had ended we just packed up our equipment and went home. The next day, after thinking about it while driving home, it was pretty impressive what we had accomplished. We had helped a spirit to cross over, who had passed, didn't know where to go and had been "stuck" here for almost 80 years. He had been reunited with family members and loved ones.

Conclusion: Not much more can be said than what is in the story. I believe that the spirit we had crossed over was the one that caused the activity in the house. The activity had stopped after we left so it's a safe bet that it was the gentleman causing the activity. We think he was causing the activity to get attention or trying to get help for himself. Whether or not you believe the investigation is your right as a reader. I was there, I have seen the pictures, and I have no reason to second guess what transpired that night. If we did indeed help him crossover we should feel good that we helped a lost soul continue his journey like he was meant to do. If we helped him to see his family again that he hasn't seen for years then we have done our job and I think we did it well in this case.

The EMF Experience...

Date: 05-31-03
Location: House in Durand

The house in question was built in the 1930's. The house was bought by the owner in 1966, and there has been at least one death in the house. Alice and Ruthie, the mother and daughter who live in the house had used an Ouija Board in the house, which may or may not have any affect on the activity they have experienced. Some of the things they have experienced include feeling cold spots, smells coming from the kitchen that includes cookies baking and coffee brewing, Ruthie hears voices that can be heard but she can't make out what is being said, upstairs light turning on and off, and the dogs will not stay outside and they sometimes look at something in the living room and will frantically bark at something that Alice and Ruthie cannot see.

The investigation started out like all the others that we have done over the years, we got some last minute information from Alice, and then Alice and Ruthie gave us a tour of the house. We came in the house through the front door and we found ourselves in a small room, similar to a coat room Directly in front of you and a little to the left was the stairs leading to the second floor. You had some stairs, then a small landing on your right, a few more stairs, and then you were in the hallway. To your left is the bathroom and right in front of you is a bedroom. If you go right, at the end of the hall is another bedroom.

If you go back down the stairs and turn left you are back in the living room. Continue into the living room and to your left is the dining room. Once in the dining room and to your left is the kitchen. There is a door on the right that leads to the backyard and a door way to your left that leads to a small hallway which then continues to the basement stairs. If you are heading to the basement, a few feet past the kitchen down the hallway, on your right is a door that leads to the driveway outside. If you continue straight down the small hallway you hit some stairs. At the bottom of the stairs you are in the main room in the basement. To your right, 20 feet or so away, is a door that leads to the furnace. If you go to your right 40 feet there is a laundry room. Right next to the laundry room is a small room used for storage. The rest of the basement is open space with boxes stacked in the corners. Overall the basement is just one big empty room. On the wall furthest from the stairs, smack dab in the center of the wall, were 2 windows that looked to the south. These 2 small windows let in some light but not enough to see with.

After our tour of the house we decided that the two most active spots would be the upstairs hall and the basement. We set up one video camera upstairs and the other one downstairs in the basement. Since we were going to spend most of the time in the basement we also decided to put a motion detector upstairs also. This would alert us to any movement by giving off an audible chime, which will get annoying after awhile. In the basement we also had four EMF detectors set up. They were sitting on boxes a few feet from the 2 basement windows. We had them arranged in a semi circle within about two-three feet apart. EMF stands for Electro Magnetic Field. We have meters that will detect changes in the EMF field. Every living thing, as well as any man made items like outlet boxes, fans, air conditioners all give off energy and cause spikes in the EMF field. Spirits are thought to be pure energy and thus they also will disrupt the EMF field and cause higher than normal readings. Our EMF meters pick up this change in the EMF field and alerts us to possible paranormal activity.

It was reported that the dogs refused to stay outside we decided to walk around the backyard, take a few readings and pictures, and see if we could get anything. There was a birdhouse that was about 15-20 feet off the ground. Scott, a member of the group, took some temperature readings with Raytek's non contact digital thermometers. If you are not familiar with this instrument it shoots out a laser beam and whatever the beam touches the device gives you an instant temperature reading of that object. Well, the odd thing is it was the end of May and if you have ever lived in Michigan you know that it still can be cold. It was chilly, about 50 degrees but not too bad. When we took a reading on the birdhouse with the Raytek, the temperature came back -10 degrees. This seemed odd so we turned it off and turned it back on and then we took another reading. We got the same temperature reading. Charles snapped a few pictures and on one of the pictures we had a good picture of Ectoplasmic mist. We wondered if it could have been Charles' breath that appeared on the picture and not real Ectoplasmic mist. I was personally right behind Charles and he held his breathe, according to protocol, and then took the picture. I saw no breath when the picture was taken. Why was the birdhouse so cold? We wish we knew. It was made of wood but it still would not have been that cold to register a -10 degrees.

During our time outside we had the video camera's running inside. When we were all outside the house was empty so there would be nothing to set off the motion detectors, also it would reduce the possibility of us getting the dreaded orb video that turned out to be dust.

Since we had been outside for about ½ hour we decided to walk around the inside of the house again to see if the energy had changed or shifted location. We started with the upstairs first. The middle bedroom felt a little different than it did before. You could actually feel the electricity in the air. It literally made the hairs on your arm stand up. We took a few pictures in the room and checked the rest of the upstairs. Nothing felt any different in the rest of the upstairs so we went downstairs to check the first floor.

We had a motion detector set up in the living room near the TV. At one point while we were upstairs it went off. We were all upstairs so I knew that none of us could have set off the motion detectors. That happens sometimes when you set up a motion detector, someone will accidentally walk in front of it. It is really comical to watch when that happens because you have 3-5 members converging on the area, all the while snapping away with the cameras. We are at a point now that we tell people it's okay if you set it off just note it on the recording that you did it. This saves us a lot of misunderstandings. The first floor was quiet so we decided to set up shop in the basement. We all trudged down there to just sit and see what happened.

We had only been in the basement for a few minutes when the activity started. Brad, one of our members but not me, was standing in the doorway leading to the laundry room. We were all standing well away from him on the other side of the basement when he jumped and immediately turned around. We were taken back by his actions and asked him what had happened and if he was okay. He said that he was standing there getting ready to take a picture and he felt someone tap him on the shoulder. The only problem was that there was no one behind him to tap him on his shoulder. This unnerved him a little bit but as they say "No harm no foul," and "The show must go on."

The EMF meters we had set up near the 2 basement windows started to register EMF spikes. We checked if there was a logical explanation for this, but we couldn't find any power boxes, wires, or anything that caused the spikes. We were averaging 2.5 - 3.2. This is in the range of paranormal activity so we started to take pictures in the area.

It was also near the windows that Scott started to feel a presence. He said it started with a headache, then the static electricity feeling. We did a quick temperature check and the area was 5-10 degrees cooler than the rest of the basement. We then checked to make sure that there wasn't a draft from the windows and there were no detectable drafts. He thought the spirit was that of a little girl. He didn't get a name or anything just the distinct impression that it was a little girl that was down there with us.

We still had the video camera recording downstairs and the 4 EMF's were still arranged in a semi circle about 2-3 feet apart. We had them facing the window where we had the high EMF readings, the temperature drop, and the impression of a little girl.

We were just standing around talking, when we decided to start trying to get EVP's. EVP stands for Electronic Voice Phenomenon. In a nut shell, it is the idea of getting voices on a recording device that was not present at the time you were recording with your device. You have to be careful though because not all voices will turn out to be EVP. Tape recorders are very sensitive and they can and will pick up voices from other rooms. If you ever have tried to get them you know that it has to be totally quiet in order to get good results. Since the group likes to talk, and I like to do my fair share of talking, sometimes getting EVP's is hard to do. We did actually have quiet for 10-15 minutes but upon playback we didn't seem to get any EVP's that night.

Someone suggested that we try to get an EVP again but this time ask it questions. Maybe we would get a response back. We asked the usual questions like "Who is here?," "Did you die here?," "What's your name?" and things along this line of questioning. After around 10 minutes of doing this you could actually feel the energy beginning to rise. I know everybody felt it even though no one actually said anything but just the looks on their faces you knew that they felt something was happening to. Then all of a sudden the EMF's started going off, the ones we had at the time all give an audible beep and the on button lights up red. They didn't all go off at the same time mind you but the farthest one away went off. By going off I don't mean turning off but beeping and the on button flashing red, then the next one, then the next one, and finally the one closest to us, until they were all beeping and flashing red. Then all of a sudden nothing, they were all totally silent. It wasn't like when they came on and they started beeping one by one, this time they all stopped beeping all at the same time, instantaneously.

I would like to use the example of a shock wave to help give you a visual. When a shock wave comes at you it isn't all at once, but you can see it coming, like we did with the EMF's, then once it hits you it is over. It was pretty impressive. We hadn't seen anything like it before and haven't seen the likes of it again since. After this happened it was absolutely quiet, no one was saying a word. We all just stood there with our mouths open, not knowing what exactly to say. Finally someone said something like "What the heck was that" or something similar. Then we all just started chiming in with our views and ideas of what we just experienced. We really did not have a readily available answer because like I said earlier, we just never had this experience before. We talked among ourselves for a few minutes and then continued with the investigation.

Nothing else happened in the basement for the rest of the investigation. We did a check of the first and second floors, nothing was to be found. We decided to call it a night. We thanked Alice and Ruthie, packed up our stuff, said our closing prayer and we went home.

Conclusion- Other than the EMF's going off at the same time and the strange temperature reading on the birdhouse outside, we didn't get anything concrete to support the claim of paranormal activity. But I would say that the things that did happen would be enough to give some validity to the claim. You could write off the birdhouse as maybe weak batteries, maybe the wood of the birdhouse somehow was cooler than the night air. Maybe, but you would have a hard time explaining the episode with the EMF's all coming on one by one, then off all at once. We have never seen this happen before or since. We don't really know what happened in the basement. Might it have been a spirit that had just enough energy to set them off, but not appear to us? Could it have been the spirit reacting to our questions but had no other way to answer them. The possibilities are endless and I will not try to list all of them here in this space. I will let you make your own decision on this one.

Catching a Train...

Date: 10-15-02
Location: Train depot in Durand

This investigation was conducted at the Old Union Train Station. It now has been converted into offices and a gift shop / museum. The building itself is huge, about 4 times long as it is wide. It has two floors and an attic. The building runs East/West. There is also a building directly behind the main building no more than 5-10 feet away that was used at one time for the baggage that the passengers would have with them on the trains. We had full access to the building and associated buildings. We did another investigation a year later and that one was an all night one. This one focus's on the first year done in 2003. For this investigation we had a newspaper reporter from a local publication, also attending was a reporter and cameraman from TV-6 in Lansing was at the investigation to tape a piece to be aired on that nights broadcast.

Let me tell you a little about the history of the train depot before I get too much further. The train depot was designed by Spier and Rohms and originally built in 1903. Eighteen months later, it was almost completely destroyed by fire and was rebuilt in 1905. During the 1900's when the railroad industry was at its peak, 42 passenger trains, 22 mail trains, and 78 freight trains passed through Durand daily. The building contained a formal dining room and a snack counter with swivel stools. You could also buy comic books selling for a nickel and buy a newspaper from a nearby newsboy. A large postal box collected the mail, which was sent by rail to its destination. The second floor of the building held railroad offices and a sleeping area for train crews. Amtrak still uses the train station and it makes daily stops on its routes to Toronto and Chicago. As a personal note, I had relatives that worked for the Grand Truck Railroad (GTW), and they actually used to work at this depot. As a boy, I remember taking the passenger train to Durand and standing near the old steam engine that still stands near the station today just like it did many years ago.

We met at a local restaurant before heading over to the train depot, as per our custom. We were looking forward to the night's investigation. We have always wanted to investigate the train station and we finally got the chance. We would be using all of our resources for this one. All of the equipment that we had would be utilized.

When you first turn the corner on Main Street and the depot is on the right, you almost feel intimidated by it. It is a big building with peeks on the corners, like a castle. You have to turn down a few more streets to get to the parking lot. The building is more impressive close up than it was from the street. If you just sit there, it's not hard to see the people from an era gone by, all going about their business. If they were either staying in Durand or if they had a layover before they caught another train to some far away destination, it was like organized chaos.

We were given the tour by Melinda. She works in the train station and was our contact for this investigation. She told us stories about how many people have had experiences in and around the buildings. She told us that co-workers will not for anything go into certain areas after dark or by themselves. People have actually seen the ghost of a female, they think she was a passenger, and of hearing footsteps upstairs when no one living was on the second floor.

When you first enter the main building, you are standing in a small foyer. To your front and a little to the right are the stairs that will take you upstairs to the second level. To your left was the dining room / snack counter. Off of this room was the kitchen, with its mandatory "In" and "Out" doors. This room is now used as the museum / gift shop and the old kitchen is now used for storage. If you leave the old dining room/snack room and continue down the long hallway you come to a big room at the extreme east end of the building. This room housed the ticket window and waiting room. Ahead of you at the end of the room is the ticket window complete with the bars that separate the train employees and the customers. Between the doors that you used to enter the room and the ticket windows are 4 sets of wooden benches to sit on. These benches were about 10 feet long. They have high backs and side panels at each end of the bench. I guess they had the high sides so people wouldn't slide off the ends of the bench.

If you just entered this room, to your left and go until you come to the wall is a door that leads to the ladies room. But this is not your ordinary bathroom. When you first enter the room you are in a lounging area. Complete with a fireplace and couch, then through another door is the bathroom. This turned out to be the most active room during the investigation. If you make your way back out of the ladies room and turn right and continue to the doors, take a right and continue until you hit the stairs, which will be the stairs that take you to the second floor. Go up the stairs and you will be standing on the second floor. To your left the hallway continues and it opens up into a large ballroom, this was once office space but they took them out years ago to make this big ballroom area. To your right the hallway continues until it opens into another room. This room is now used for storage. There is a door in the ceiling right before you enter the storage room, you will need a ladder to get into the attic, which runs the whole length of the building, since there is no built in stairs into the attic. On both sides of the hallway there are numerous rooms that are used for offices. If you go back downstairs to the front door and exit, turn right, and follow the main building to the end, then walk a few feet, you will come to the baggage room. This is divided up into 3 different rooms, covering 2 floors. The main floor is where the scales were and to the right was the office area. Straight ahead are the stairs that go down to the basement level. Downstairs was used to store the baggage. There is also a room dedicated to model trains, this being in the far end of the main building, but you have to go outside of the main building, and walk towards the baggage room. Right near the end of the main building is a door that will take you to this room. The room is big and divided up into two sections. The one section had memorabilia dedicated to trains, where the other section has a big operating train set that goes through mountains, over a stream, and into an imaginary town.

After the tour was completed we unpacked the equipment and talked about where we wanted to have everything set up. We decided to put one camcorder in the hallway upstairs and one in the original room upstairs that is now used as storage. We did put one camcorder in the ladies room downstairs, but we did not start using monitors yet so we had to be in there in order to see what was occurring.

Charles, one of our members, set up his camera in the storage room. He set up his monitor in the ball room at the other end of the hall. We put one of our cameras in the ladies room, along with a motion detector and the Trifield EMF. We also added a motion detector in the upstairs hall.

This is basically all we do. We set up our equipment and watch and see what happens. Sound like fun? Most of the things we get are due to luck. If the spirits can indeed hear you, they know our intentions. If they don't want to show themselves, they won't.

Our first event of the evening happened near the ticket booth in the waiting room. Three of our members, Brenda, Mary and Karen, were in the room with the ticket booths, in the general area of the ladies room when Karen saw something come out of the wall about

25 feet from them. Either Brenda or Mary saw what Karen did because they were looking in a different direction. Karen described what she saw as a shadow, but it was definitely a person. She couldn't make out any features but Karen thought from its height that it was probably was a male. Karen said that it came out from the wall, walked 10-15 feet, and then totally disappeared before her eyes. Karen felt that it was nothing to be afraid of but it just caught her by surprise. It had caught all three of them off guard so much that they had no time to take a picture to try and get it on film. Karen said that she was more focused on watching the shadow than trying to get a picture. This is totally understandable.

Nothing of much interest happened upstairs. We didn't get anything on video and only had a few good positive pictures. This happens sometimes. It really is a hit or miss chance for opportunities like this.

Something of interest did happen out in the baggage room that is worth mentioning. We had five members go out there with a couple of cameras and an EMF meter. There is a heavy door that slides shut, which is the main door to get into the baggage room. They had opened the door to gain access to the room and they went downstairs. They didn't get too much there so they headed back up to the main floor. They were just getting ready to leave the baggage room and go back into the depot when they had the door slam shut on them. You have to understand that this is a very heavy door and there is no way this could have closed on its own accord. Something or someone would have to close it. They told me over the two way radios what had happened and that they were a little freaked with what had just occurred. I checked to make sure that everyone was okay, which they were, so I told them to make a log of it and come back into the depot. They said okay and opened the door to exit the building. That's when it happened. When they opened the door, there in front of them stood three people, they started laughing so hard that our members knew they were up to no good. It turns out that they are train watchers. They come down to the train depot every night and watch the trains go by. They are harmless, but they couldn't resist pulling a practical joke on our members and they are the ones that closed the door. So needless to say after this little unwanted attention, whenever anyone went into the baggage room again that night they were to post a guard at the door to make sure that the train watching people didn't get the same idea as before.

We did have a couple of area's that we did get what is called "Psychic Impressions." This is where people who are mediums or psychics, the words are interchangeable, get impressions about either people or events. Whether or not you believe in this is up to you but I will tell you what we got in the train depot as far as impressions go.

The first one was in the ladies room. More specifically it was in the ladies waiting room. I am not trying to be funny about this but it sounds funny when I read it also. Linda, one of our mediums and a good friend, picked up a female presence in the waiting room. She thought that the woman fell ill on the train but didn't die there. The other passengers, along with the train employees, brought her into the ladies room and put her on the couch. They attended to her the best they could but not knowing what was wrong with her they could do very little for her but they made her as comfortable as possible. We feel that she passed in the ladies room. For whatever reason she is still in there.

The second place would be in the baggage room, but only in the lower lever. This was where they handled and stored most of the baggage that came off the trains. Linda felt the physical pain that would go with someone who had to work hard, long hours picking up and handling baggage. Linda also felt that the person had a bad back and also his shoulders were drooping like they also hurt. She also picked up the presence of a Native American. This person might have worked for the railroad or he might have been just passing through.

Conclusion- Just based on the history alone this place has had so many people come through it, either on business or pleasure, that there has to be a few spirits that have stayed on the grounds. We didn't get anything proof positive on film, but the experiences we had lead us to believe that the depot does indeed have a few spirits lingering around the building.

Double Trouble...

Date: 01-10-04
Location: House in Haslett

This one actually turned into an opportunity that most investigators don't get and one we couldn't pass up.

We had done an investigation in Lansing years earlier, and the homeowner of that home is friends with the homeowner of this home, we will call her Maggie, and she was experiencing activity so she was looking for a ghost hunting group to come to her home and conduct an investigation. The two were talking one day when the conversation turned to ghosts. Don't ask me how because the topic isn't something that you can ease into easily. Anyhow the homeowner who we did an earlier investigation for told Maggie about us and gave her our web address.

Maggie went online to our website and submitted an investigation request. This is how most investigations start. The person wanting us to come out must first fill out an investigation request form on our website and part of that request is to list some of the activity they were experiencing. The questions get more in depth on the questionnaire, this is a form that is filled out online, before the actual investigation can take place. We like a little more history before we make contact. Some of the things they were experiencing were knocking sounds on the walls, sounds of water running, and sounds of crying and laughter.

Maggie told us that her family had also seen the spirit in their living room. He was sitting on the couch dressed in a red flannel shirt so they named him "Red" and that is what they called him from that point on whenever they saw him. They said that Red wasn't harmful they just felt like he was picking on them by hiding things and turning things on and off. The family had a dog that also would react to Red. It would look at something that no one could see and follow movement with his eyes.

The investigation was in January and it was the first one of the year. We have a standing tradition that if the investigation is close to us we have everyone over to our house for dinner and then we head off to the investigation. This one was close enough so we ordered pizza and talked about the upcoming investigation. When the investigation time came closer we packed up the van and headed to the house to conduct the evening's investigation.

January in Michigan can be brutal and this night was one of them. It was around 18 degrees outside, but thankfully little wind. We hurriedly went into the house to get warm. Maggie gave us the customary tour of the house and again we made notes of the spots where we picked up something, and finished the tour. We brought in the equipment at this point and started to unpack everything.

The house was a two story with a basement. There are 2 bedrooms upstairs and 1 down. There were 2 doors that you used to get into the house. There was a front door in the living room and a back door that opened up into a coat room, just off the kitchen. That is the door that we used. Straight ahead was the stairs that took you down into the basement. To your left was the kitchen / dining room area. Walk a few feet and to your left was a downstairs bedroom. If you continued walking straight a few feet and you would come to the living room. In the far right corner of the living room were the stairs that took you up to the second floor. Once upstairs you were standing in a small bedroom. If you walked straight ahead you would eventually be standing in the master bedroom. The eldest son had a bedroom in the basement. Like so many homes we have investigated over the years this house was just your ordinary home.

After our walk through we decided to put one camcorder upstairs in the hallway along with a motion detector and Trifield EMF and the camcorder in the living room. This one was the wireless camera. We also had a recorder upstairs to try and record EVP. We also used our temperature monitoring equipment because we felt that the upstairs was a little cooler than the rest of the house. If anything were to happen we wanted to document any temperature changes that might occur.

Before I give you the details on what happened during the investigation lets flash back to the tour that was given by the homeowner and what happened that is worth mentioning. We were in the basement bedroom. Off of the bedroom is a storage area. They had a headboard that had a mirror attached to it. There was nothing special about the headboard but when you walked in front of it and put your hand in front of the mirror you could feel the energy coming off of it! I asked Linda, one of our members, if she could feel it and she said that she could. We asked where they had acquired the headboard and they said that it came from a place they used to live. Then out of nowhere came to me the name of "Oscar." I also felt he had died of a stroke. They said that it didn't ring a bell with them. We let it go at that but asked them to just remember the name and if they thought of anything else to let us know. Meanwhile feeling that they key to most of the activity was connected to this headboard. We felt so strongly about this that we suggested that they either move the headboard outside or get rid of it. The energy coming off this headboard was electrifying.

Since we had set up a camcorder in the upstairs bedroom, a few of us decided to go up there and watch the camera to see if we would get anything. The homeowner also joined us. She was saying that

Red did this and Red did that. It was accepted that Red was there but other than the time they saw him sitting on the couch they never saw him again. We weren't upstairs for more than 15 minutes when the orbs started to show up on video. We had the master bedroom and part of the bedroom we were in sealed off, so no one was entering these rooms. The dust theory would be thrown out of the equation. I looked over to Maggie and she had this quizzical look on her face. I asked her what was wrong and she said that they knew that they had a spirit in the house but to actually see them in real time on the camcorder moving through the upstairs was unnerving and made her a little scared. We told her that there was nothing to worry about and that they couldn't hurt her. Just as we said that, the Trifield EMF went off, and it was only five feet from us sitting on the desk.

While we were upstairs Maggie called a friend to let her know that we had started the investigation and there was some activity going on in the house. Maggie told her friend that we got the name Oscar and that she had no idea whom that was. Then all of a sudden during her conversation, she said "Oh my God, you are right." We waited for her to end the call before we asked her what she found out. She said that she totally forgot about this but when they lived up North they lived with a family friend and that his name was Oscar. We also found out that he had died from a stroke and the headboard that they have had came from the same bed that Oscar used to sleep in. It took a phone call to bring the memory of Oscar back. Coincidence? Lucky guess?

While we were upstairs with the video cameras the orbs that we saw were all going into the master bedroom and going into the corner and disappearing. We suspected that there might be a portal to the other side and that the spirits were coming through there. Unfortunately we had no idea where they were going to. We had been in the house for 3 hours and the activity was slowing down so there was little or nothing happening in the house. The consensus among the group was that we had a good investigation but maybe we should bring it to a close. We packed up all of the equipment and put everything back in the vehicles. We asked Maggie and her family if they wanted us to clean the house and they were not sure. They didn't want to make "Red" mad so they were undecided. We told them that since we were close by, if they changed their minds, we would be more than happy to come back and clean the house for them.

Five months later we received another investigation request from Maggie. Our first thought was that the activity had gotten worse and they wanted us to come back out. We were way off on this one. It turns out the house next door was empty and their family also owned that house. Maggie wanted to know if we wanted to investigate the empty house next door since they had been in the house and felt things there also. Seeing what a golden opportunity this was we graciously accepted the invitation.

We assembled the team and headed out to the investigation site. The empty house is indeed just across the driveway from the house we had already investigated. This other house is a two story home with a bedroom upstairs. We entered the house through the back door, and we were in the kitchen/dining room area. Straight ahead was the living room. The stairs leading to the upstairs was on your left, just a little ways into the living room. There was a front door at the far end of the room. If you went up the stairs you came to a small landing. On your left was a small bedroom. If you followed the hallway all the way around you would come to a closet that was on your right. As we stated before, the house was empty of furniture and people, we had the full run of both houses. We did a quick walk through of this house and we sensed that there was indeed a portal in the house and our best estimate was that the portal was upstairs in the hallway. We set up video cameras in both houses hoping that maybe the portal went between the houses and we had hoped to get something concrete to prove this fact. We split up the team, half in the house we had already investigated, and the other half in the new house. We had two-way radios so we could communicate between teams if the occasion presented itself.

Since we had already investigated the first house we didn't spend much time going through it again. We didn't feel there was a need since we weren't there to investigate the house this time anyways. We did look in on the headboard and it was gone! We asked Maggie where the headboard went and she told us that right after the first investigation they gave it away. We told them that it was probably a good idea that they did.

Everything was ready. We had two video cameras set up, one was in each house. We still hadn't added the video monitors yet so we had to watch the video from the screen on the cameras. In the first house we investigated, we again were seeing orbs in the master bedroom and again they were still going into the corner by the dresser. We had something happen that was pretty interesting and it might have substantiated our claim of a portal. We had a particularly bright orb that went from the room that we were in to the master bedroom and into the corner, and then it was gone. A few seconds after it disappeared from our house, we received a call on the 2-way radios from the other house saying that a bright orb just came in over there and it came from the wall in the hallway right in front of the closet. The best thing here is that both video cameras were recording and we have both orbs, in two different houses, all of it on tape. We looked at both videos and the orb looks the same. But, and this is a big but, there isn't any features that would help distinguish the two from each other. So we can't be sure if they were indeed the same orb.

It seems that the portal in the other house was either in the back of a closet, or was nearer the front. In either case there was a portal that connected the two homes. At one point Linda sensed that something was trying to get through the portal and enter the house. Since she was standing right next to the closet door it couldn't complete the trip. She sensed that it was non-human spirit. She described it as a really big creature. She didn't sense anything evil about it, but we didn't need to have it come into the house. Linda did attempt to close the portal and she thinks she was successful in doing so.

While we were upstairs in the second house we did get some impressions in the only bedroom on the second floor. A few of us kept getting the images of livestock. The only thing that we can think of is that the house used to be a barn and it was converted into a house later. We were seeing pigs, cows, and chickens. We also had an image of a young man in bib overalls and that killed himself there. Probably when it was a barn because we "saw" him hanging from high beams like the kind you would find in barns. He was not a particularly nice person and maybe all the anger that he might have had in life is still there in death, never to diminish. After staying in both homes for well over 3 hours the activity again was almost non-existent. The group agreed that it would a good time to end the investigation. We again packed up the equipment and put it in the van

We thanked Maggie for letting us into her home once again and for giving us access to the other house. We had an opportunity that not too many groups get and we were thankful for the chance.

Conclusion-We believe that both houses had some kind of activity in it. The first house that we did had one that they called Red and we believe that Oscar was also there. We believe that the second house was a barn of some type originally, but sometime over the years was converted into a house. This is where we had the image of a young man that had killed himself years before when it was a barn structure of some type. The activity is nothing that is going to hurt anyone but is more of an annoyance that makes you wonder if this is actually happening or are you losing your mind type of thing.

Ready to Check Out...

Date: 09-21-02
Location: Store in Owosso

We actually got to do an investigation in this store because the owners are members of the group. After they joined they offered to have us come in and do an investigation. They said that things had been going on there for years and never had anyone else come in. When we had an opening in our schedule we took them up on their offer to investigate their store. We have been in there a total of 2 times but I will just cover the first investigation that we did there. John and Mona, the owners of the store, have recently moved up north and the store has been sold.

The building itself has been in Mona's family for many years, if I remember correctly, they have owned it since the 1920's. The building is much older than that but I believe that is when the family took it over. It isn't big by today's standards but it is more geared to be like a convenience store. It carries everything from meat, to boxed goods, from fruits to bread and everything in between. It is a nice store for the area as it would save you the hassle of driving to a nearby town to purchase things at a big box store.

The store consists of a good sized main shopping area and coolers for beer and pop at the front of the store. At the back of the store, they have a good selection of meats and the aisles are neatly arranged and stocked. Behind the scenes, there is a small employee break room right near the door by the coolers and near the loading docks is an area for empty bottles and cans to be kept until they are picked up. The basement is full sized, has a cement floor, and used mainly for storage. There is an old knife sharpening wheel in the basement and we will tell you more about what happened with that old grinding wheel shortly.

We like to hear some of the things that are going on before we go to a site for an investigation. Some of the stories we heard about this store were really amazing. They are amazing not because we don't believe them but because they happened to customers and workers alike, and the scope of the things that they have experienced are really interesting. Here are some of the stories were heard.

The first event happened in the basement. The basement just has a strange feeling about it, nothing frightening or hazardous, just like there is something down there with you. Case in point. They would have workers from utility companies go into the basement to take meter readings. As the owners would get comfortable with the utility workers they would tell them some of the activity that was going on down there. Not so much as to frighten them but to give them a heads up, if you will, so they would know what to expect while in the basement and to keep their eyes open for odd things. There is a door that opens off the back storage room, and leads into the basement. The light switch is at the top of the stairs just inside the door. The stairs leading down to the basement are very steep and if you are tall and not careful you will get a major headache courtesy of the low ceiling at the bottom of the stairs. I know this from a very painful experience and had a bump on my forehead to prove it. One of the workers went into the basement to get a meter reading when all of a sudden he came barreling up the stairs, broke the light switch trying to turn it off, and high tailed it to his truck outside. John and Mona happened to be in the back room and caught up with him and asked him what had happened to make him react the way he did. He said that he was in the corner reading the meter, which he has done numerous times before in the store. He said that he felt like he wasn't alone in the basement even though he knew that he was. There is a heavy old fashioned grinding wheel that was used in the old days to grind knives. It is the kind that has a seat and you sit down on it. There are two pedals that make the wheel turn, much like a modern day exercise bike. So you sit down and put your feet on the pedals and pedal. This causes the wheel to turn and you put the knife against the wheel while it is turning and the knife gets sharpened. You can't turn the wheel easily, it is pretty heavy. Now let's get back to the worker. He said that he was about 10 feet from the wheel when it started to turn by itself. The worker said that he didn't wait around to see what happened next and that he had no plans on going back down there again in the foreseeable future, or at least until the next meter read.

This next incident involves a customer that had no prior knowledge of the activity in the store and it happened in the main shopping area. Some of the workers of the store saw this woman come in and she grabbed one of those little shopping baskets, the ones with the plastic handles. She was going down the aisles and putting things in her basket. She was just your average shopper. After 10-15 minutes of shopping the woman came up to the check-out to pay for her items. This is when she asked the workers if they knew there was a ghost in the store and that it was unhealthy to keep a cat in a grocery store. They knew that the store had a spirit or two but was certain there were no pets in the store. They asked what had happened. She said that she shopping the next to the last aisle. She asked herself out loud "Where the cake mixes would be?" She heard a female voice, the customer said that it sounded like the person was right behind her, say it's in aisle 4. She turned around to thank the person that told her but there was no one near her. In fact, besides the workers, she was the only customer in the store and the workers were at the checkout which is at the front of the store. She didn't think anything of it at the time even though she couldn't find the source of the voice and headed over to aisle 4. This is when she had her "cat" encounter. Having pets in a "mom and pop" store are not unheard of, in fact, they are getting more common than you might think. However, having food in the store, she thought is was unwise to have a pet that roams free. She said that a black cat walked right past her feet in the opposite direction that she was heading. She thought it was remarkable that a cat would walk past her without even so much as a look. The cat walked past her like she didn't even exist. She immediately looked behind her, but the cat was no where to be seen. She said only a few seconds elapsed from the time she saw the cat walk past her until she looked back at it. It was like it just vanished. The workers told the woman that customers have reported odd things that happened in the store before, but that no one had reported a cat sighting before that is until now. I think that is would be a good time to remind everyone that because the cat was black in color, it does not signify that cat as being evil or demonic. There is no direct link to black cats being demonic other than tall tales on Halloween. So please people, leave them alone. As a cat lover I must state this.

This story comes from and involves the owners, John and Mona. They were closing up one night and there was one customer left in the store. They waited for him to finish up his shopping before they locked the doors for the night. After the customer left the store they locked the door behind him and started to clean up the store. John started to close the till and Mona started to vacuum the store. Mona was near the front of the store when she noticed movement near the back of the store. She stopped the vacuum and looked up. At the back of the store was a figure, Mona thought it was a man, and it walked from the back aisle towards the door that leads to the employee area in the back room. Mona was alarmed because John was behind the front check out counting the till and there was no one else in the store. Mona told John what she saw and they both went into the area where the figure was last seen going into. To her surprise there was no one there. They searched the whole store from basement to the store area and they found no one. The doors were still locked and no windows were broken. There was no way anyone could have gotten out. Whoever she saw just vanished! Now they have seen things obviously before in the store but this is the first time they actually saw a spirit in the store. They usually just heard things and saw movement out of the corner of their eyes, but nothing like this had happened before. John and Mona told us that at the time the prospect of that person they saw being a ghost seemed remote. It looked like a living, breathing person. After our second investigation they said that they haven't seen the man since.

And finally the last story, John and Mona were stocking the shelves. They were talking about this and that when the soup cans started to fly off the shelves. Not all of them, but one, then one more, then one more. They said that a total of 5 soups cans just flew off the shelf. There was no one close enough to knock them off and no truck went by that might have caused a vibration and caused the cans to fall off the shelf. They just looked at each other and chalked it up to one of the spirits having fun with them.

Now that we have told you some of the activity they have experienced, let's get to the investigation itself. We met at a local eatery. We talked over the investigation and some of the activity that had been going on there. We told our members some of the activity but not the location where it had actually occurred. We like to see if people experience the same thing as other people have or if they get feelings in certain locations that correspond with reported activity.

We parked out back and let the owners know that we were there. They opened up the back door and we brought in our equipment. The owners gave us the customary walk through, and when the tour was over, we talked about where to put the equipment.

We decided to put a video camera down in the basement and one in the store. Charles also put his wireless camera in the basement. He set up his monitor in the hallway next to the break room. We also put a motion detector in aisle 2, the most active, and the Trifield EMF. We had members walk through the store taking EMF readings and taking pictures.

There were a couple of interesting things that happened during the investigation. The first one being that while we were in the basement, the previously fore mentioned sharpening wheel moved on its own. There were 6 of us in the basement. We had a video camera not more than 2 feet from the wheel with its aim towards us. We turned out the lights so it was pretty dark since there were no windows to let in the light from outside. We were asking questions to see if we got any response from any spirits that might be with us. I was a few feet from the wheel, and no one else was within 5 feet of it. As we were asking questions you could hear the wheel move, it made a grinding sound as it turned, it was silent for a moment and you could hear it turning again. We know what the wheel sounded like when it moved because we moved it early in the investigation. We did this because of the story that it moved on its own when the utility worker was down there reading the meter and we wanted to hear what it sounded like, in case it happened again while we were there, also we wanted to see how easily the wheel turned. The whole event lasted just a few seconds. We immediately turned our flashlights on the wheel but there was no one near it. We started taking pictures in the hope of getting something. The only way to make it move would be to actually sit down, but you would have heard the seat creaking if some one had actually sat down in the chair and that would make a totally different sound. We didn't hear a sitting down sound, just the turning sound. We looked at each other as to say did you hear the same thing I did. We all agreed that we heard it move. So we stopped the video cameras to see what was captured on tape. And sure enough, you could hear us talking, then the sound of the wheel turning then silence. There were more sounds of the wheel turning, then nothing. Then all of us talking could be heard on the tape. As odds would have it the video camera was pointing towards us and not the wheel. So all we have on video is the sound of the wheel turning, but not the wheel actually turning on its own.

The other incident that occurred was that Charles was watching the monitor with the camera set up in the basement when he heard footsteps coming from the basement. In case you were wondering how he did that, the camera had video and audio. It was transmitting video and audio to the monitor. So if anything happened in the basement he would hear and see it on the monitor upstairs. We checked to make sure that none of our members were in the basement, no one was. We were all accounted for. The prospect of us getting footsteps in the basement was exciting. We would actually get proof of a possible paranormal event. Our excitement was quickly subdued. The footsteps were from us walking upstairs. The acoustics of the basement made it sound like the footsteps were actually in the basement. I added this in here so you will understand the need to check all possible causes before you post on your website that you have caught something paranormal.

The last thing that was strange happened in aisle 2, towards the end of the investigation. We had set up the Trifield about ½ of the way down the aisle. We also had a motion detector on the middle of three shelves, facing the end of the aisle, away from us.

The motion detector can get annoying because it will sound an audible alarm, the sound is like "Ding-Dong" when motion is detected. Every so often during the investigation the motion detector would go off. During one occurrence I asked the spirits to let me photograph them. I told them I would count to 3, and take a picture. If they wanted to show themselves to us, please be in the aisle when I got to 3. Sounds silly but try it sometimes you might be surprised at what you might get on film. So I counted to three and took a picture. There was a really bright orb in the middle of the aisle. Whether or not by me asking helped in getting the results we did we may never know but it's nice to think that it.

This picture was taken in a store during an investigation. I asked the spirit to show itself to us when I counted to 3. I counted to 3 and took this picture.

Normally the motion detector will give you the audible alarm as a constant sound until the motion is stopped. But we started to notice that it would only "ding" once then stop, or twice then stop. The first thing we did was to check the batteries, they were fine. Secondly, we checked to see if any one of us could have been getting in the range of the detectors. We looked like wild men and women jumping up and down, waving our arms to see if we set it off, we didn't. We started to wonder if the spirit was trying to communicate with us. So we spoke to no one in particular that if they wanted to talk to us we would try and communicate with them. We asked the spirits to use the motion detectors on the shelf to "ding" once for "yes" and twice for "no." Surprisingly it "dinged" once. We even set up the other motion detector on the other side of the aisle, on the top shelf, to see if it to would start going off, it did. So for the next ½ hour we were asking a lot of questions, and the motion detector seemed to be the "go between" of the spirit and us during this time. We had the video cameras on us the whole time, even though we didn't see anything while this was going on, we did get it all on tape. A few days after we watched the tapes of the events and it still was amazing that it happened. We didn't get a spirit on video. I can't explain why we didn't, but we have the audio from the tape to back up our claims.

Conclusion-We believe that the store does absolutely have some kind of activity. The eyewitness accounts from the owners to customers and from what we experienced during our investigation, we would be amiss to disclaim all of this as an overactive imaginations. We had fun during our two times there and we had an open invitation to go back whenever the urge hit us. Unfortunately the owners sold the store and moved to the Upper Peninsula of Michigan. We haven't been over there to see if the store is still a store. Maybe we will drop in one day and inquire if any meter readers have broken the light switch again while making a mad dash from their basement. And we will say this with a smile on our faces of course.

A Message from a Son...

Date: 06-06-03
Location: House in Port Huron

We met at the local McDonald's. Are you seeing a pattern here to what our favorite place to eat is? We went over the night's investigation while we ate and after we were through eating our Big Mac's we headed off to a member's house, her name is Julie. The owner of the house, where the investigation was to take place, is Julie's friend and she set up the investigation for us. From Julie's house we had a 5-10 minute ride by car to her friend's house for the investigation that night.

This investigation was conducted in a charming house in the Michigan's thumb region. When you came in the front door the staircase leading upstairs is on your immediate right, with the living room off to our left. If you continued straight ahead you are in the kitchen. To your left through the kitchen is the dining area and to your right is another bathroom and a utility room. If you went up the stairs you are in the hallway upstairs. To your right is the bathroom and straight ahead is a bedroom. If you turned left and walked down the hall there is a bedroom to your right, which is the master bedroom, and the last bedroom was straight ahead at the end of the hallway.

The owner, I will call her Amy, is a mom with twin girls. Amy contacted her friend Julie, whom in turn contacted us because of the activity that was happening in the home. Some of the things Amy reported were, her cats have been trying to attack things that

113

couldn't be seen by the family, the daughters are scared to sleep in their own room because they claim that they see a man looking in the window. The only problem with this is that the bedrooms are on the second floor and there is no balcony nor is there a tree even close by the window. One time she was sitting on the couch and there was an indentation on the cushions as if someone was sitting there next to her. One of her daughters had a dream of her brother and he tells her that it was him sitting on the couch next to his mother. He passed away 1 ½ years before our investigation.

We said our hello's and brought in the equipment. The homeowner then gave us the tour of the house. We definitely felt some energy in the twins' room and the hallway upstairs. The rest of the house felt pretty normal. After the tour was finished we started to set up the equipment.

We felt that most of the activity was concentrated upstairs we decided to focus most of our attention there. We set up a video camera in the hallway and a motion detector on the stairs. We had the Trifield in the twins' bedroom and tried to get EVP in both the master bedroom and the girl's room. All of the members picked where they wanted to be and some went in the girl's room and some in the master bedroom. They were each trying to get EVP.

There were a few things that happened to us during this investigation. The first event that happened was to Linda, one of our members. Linda's cell phone was scratched but we don't think that no one alive did it. There wasn't a scratch on it when the investigation started. I personally saw the phone prior to and after the investigation and I can safely say that the scratch somehow happened while we were at the house. We did make contact with a spirit in the master bedroom and it wasn't a nice one to say the least. We think that this spirit was to blame. Linda also was carrying a tape recorder so she was actively trying to get some EVP. With most EVP's you don't hear anything until playback. She didn't listen to the tape until she was home that night. She said that I almost got a phone call during the night. She was listening to the tape and she was alone in the house. There were some disturbing things on the tape, in a man's voice. About that time her cats started freaking out and she was afraid that she brought the spirit home with her, which happens regularly to Linda unfortunately. She said a few prayers, burned some incense and things started to quiet down.

There were a couple of other things that happened but they didn't involve anything physical but it was spiritual. We had confirmation from Amy that the two spirits that we were picking up were indeed known to her, and that the possibility of them being there in the house with the family was good. The first spirit was sensed in the upstairs hall. We were right in front of the master bedroom when I suddenly felt the whole left side of my body go numb and a shooting pain in my head. I have felt this pain before during other investigations and it is usually associated with either a stroke or aneurysm. I asked that someone get Amy, who was in the living room at that time, because we needed to identify the spirit. One of our members went down to tell her we needed her upstairs because we were getting a spirit and we needed to figure out who it was. Amy came upstairs and I asked her if anybody that she knew had had a stroke. She said yes, her grandma did. I then asked her if her grandma had paralysis on her left side and she again confirmed this fact. I told her that her grandma was here and I felt that she was keeping an eye on them.

The other event happened to Linda. She kept getting a message while she was in the master bedroom. The spirit kept telling her, "I am here for you." This was repeated over and over again. The spirit obviously thought that this message was important enough to repeat it over and over again to Linda. Now comes the tricky part. Who is the message for and who is saying it? It could have been for anyone of us, or it might have been from a wayward spirit that was just passing through. We decided to start at the top and ask Amy. Linda and I found Amy sitting in the kitchen so we asked her if she knew what the message meant. As soon as the Linda told her she immediately began crying. We felt like really bad because here she is crying because of something that we said and we had no idea what it meant to her. She quickly regained her composure and told us "Thank You." This made us feel a lot better, not the heels we thought we were just a few minutes before.

She proceeded to tell us what had happened to her son. Her son was a perfectly healthy child growing up. Then he got sick, in his teens, and all we know was that it was terminal. That was all Amy told us and we didn't ask anymore about it. When he was sick his mom and his sisters were understandably upset with his condition. He was a trooper and even though he was sick and the end was near he was more concerned about Amy and his sisters than with his own health issues. He told her over and over again that "I am here for you." When we received this message upstairs in the master bedroom this proved to Amy that her son was indeed there. The son wanted his mom to know that he was there and still watching over her to make sure things was okay.

After this happened we felt pretty good about the evenings events and decided to pack things up and go home. We thanked Amy for allowing us into her home and hoped that the message that she got would help ease the pain of her son's passing.

Conclusion-We believe that both the grandma and son's spirits are in the house and either looking over or protecting them. Just the message "I am here for you" from her son that had passed says it all. We did clean the house and haven't heard how things are going over there. We assume okay since we haven't heard anything. The funny thing about the investigation is that we never did determine who the man was that was scaring the daughters so much. Maybe when we cleaned the house he moved on to a better place, or maybe he found another place haunt.

You Are Paroled, Leave...

Date: 08-21-03
Location: Prison in Mansfield Ohio

The former Ohio State Reformatory is now open for tours on Sundays and ghost hunts on week-ends. This is the one and only place where I have actually seen an apparition during an investigation.

This prison was built in the 1800's and served as a training camp during the civil war. It started out as a youth training center but later was turned into a prison for adults. The prison was open until 1991 and over 150,000 inmates went through her gates. There have been, as you could imagine, some deaths between her walls. Some have been as simple as old age or natural causes but some more brutal like murders. One guard was killed while in the guard house on the roof and we know of at least two inmates that were killed in the prison.

Even the warden's wife wasn't immune from the dangers of living in a prison. In the warden's quarters, more specifically in the bedroom, there is a nice walk in closet with drawers on both sides. The warden kept a loaded pistol in the top drawer for protection. One day his wife was reaching to get something and the gun dropped to the floor and discharged. The wife was shot in the torso and fell to the ground. They waited until the orderlies came before they took her to the infirmary, where sadly, she died. The cause of the death was officially declared an accident but there are many rumors abound that the warden killed her after they got into an argument.

Some say that justice was served years later when the warden himself dropped dead of a heart attack while working at his desk. I talked to some of the volunteers at the prison and they all think that there is more to this story than meets the eye. They say that from where she was shot, the angle, her wounds, would all suggest that it didn't happen the way that the report says it did. But this is just their thoughts and it doesn't convey the feelings of the people who own the prison.

We didn't even know that such a place existed until Dennis had a magazine from Ohio and the prison was featured in it. They hold an annual Halloween event, and then from April-November they hold twice a month ghost hunts. The ghost hunts last from 8PM-6AM the following morning. There is no electricity in the prison so it is totally dark inside after the sun goes down, adding to the creepiness of the prison. They serve a late dinner of pizza and pop at 11PM and then you are off again. They close the main gates (for cars) at promptly 8PM and they only open them back up for a short time on the hour for those that wish to leave. The gates are closed again until the next hour comes along. We have been going there once a year ever since, this year (2008) marks our 6th time going down there. The drive from our home is a little over 3 hours. We usually meet at a local eatery for a quick meal before heading to the prison.

Once you are at the prison you have to go into the building that was the old gift shop and check in. If I failed to mention it before you need to be at least 21 years of age to get into the prison. During check in they do check your ID and then they give you one of those paper bracelets to wear on your wrist. This shows that you paid your money and that you are there for the hunt you signed up for. After you check in you can wander the grounds. There is however a working prison behind the prison that is used for the ghost hunts and they frown on you getting too close to it. You can hang out in your car or visit the gift shop until 8PM, that's when the ghost hunt officially starts.

A few minutes before 8PM the person in charge of that nights ghost hunt calls everyone over to the front porch area and they give you the ground rules for the evenings hunt. They tell you what you can do, can't do, where to go, places to stay out of.

After the ground rules have been told to everyone in attendance, they will assemble the people attending the ghost hunt into small groups. The staff will then take the groups into the prison and show them where the current hot spots for activity have been, stories of events that have happened in the prison, and some will tell you personal stories of their experiences in the prison.

They do give you maps of the prison so that will help you to navigate the many halls and rooms. After everyone has been on the tour of the inside they bring you all back to the outside near the front porch. The staff will then turn off the lights and open the doors. At this time you are free to go in and go anywhere your little heart desires. Some people have a game plan and they want to go here first, then there. Most people however just start walking and they go wherever the urge takes them and when they get lost, wherever the hallway takes them. There is a saying when you are in the prison and that is "Go away from the light." This means that when you get lost, look out an exterior window, if you see lights from the working prison go the opposite way and you will find your way back to the free world.

Since we have been there before we know what areas we want to go to first. Just remember that it is going to be a long night. There is no hurry in getting to a certain place. This year they told us they opened the infirmary up for the first time and the west guard shack was also opened for the first time. So we made sure to check these places out first, just to see what kind of "vibe" we got.

To try and give you an idea about the size of this place is impossible. It is just plain big. If you want to see some of the prison without actually making the trip down there, numerous movies have been filmed on location in the prison or on the grounds. The best known I think is "Shawshank Redemption." There was also "Tango and Cash," "Air Force One," and "Harry Goes to Washington." The best view of the prison is in "Shawshank Redemption," when the plane flies over the prison grounds. If you have seen the movie you know what scene I am referring to, and if you haven't, I would recommend that you do see it before heading down. The walls that surround the prison in the movie are gone, so are the buildings that once were inside the walls. The only building left of the original layout are the cells blocks and administration sections.

The prison sat empty for a few years. The state was planning to tear it down when a group of people formed a committee to raise money to save the grand old place. They saw the prison more for its historical values than it just being an eye sore. They bought the buildings for $1. Over the years that it was unoccupied the building fell into disrepair. There were holes in the windows and roof which caused a lot of water damage. Not to mention the birds, bats, and raccoons that decided to call the prison home. The stone exterior started to crumble, wallpaper was peeling, and tons of paint that, left unattended for years, was flaking off the walls and ceiling.

I won't get into the whole time spent at the prison because it would take way too long. Over the years the best spots for activity have been the warden's quarters and isolation, commonly referred to as solitary confinement. Of course though, any place in the prison has the possibility of being active on any given night and time. We all had the feelings at different times and in different places of being watched, that something was with us, and hearing footsteps. In all of the years that we have been going to the prison we have never once been physically attacked. We have been touched a few times but that is the extent of the physical contact. And then it was more of just a tap on the shoulder just to let you know that you are not alone. As a matter of fact, I have yet to hear about an incident where someone has actually been physically attacked. Most of the reports I have been hearing are of people getting pictures of orbs, some video, hearing things and at times EVP.

Other than the above mentioned feelings, we have had a couple of interesting things happen to us while at the prison. At this time we would like to thank the volunteers and members of the board that have helped us over the years by putting up with our endless amount of questions, showing us places that we had heard about but didn't know where they were and honoring our request to allow us to bring in all of our equipment and use the electrical outlets for the equipment that needed to be plugged in. Here are a few of the experiences that we have had over the years at the ghost hunts. They are in no particular order.

Our first year attending the ghost hunts was in 2001. We had 6 members make the trip down with us. We were very excited because it was our first time investigating the prison.

We have done hundreds of investigations over our 12 years of existence as a group but that first trip to the prison still holds a dear spot in our hearts. We were on the front porch near the admin section of the prison eating our pizza diner and we had overheard one of the volunteers telling some of the other ghost hunters how to get to the wardens quarters. After he was finished with them, we asked him how to get to solitary confinement, which was one of the places we had wanted to go to. He started telling us how to get there and we must have had the deer in a headlight look on our face. He was giving us directions but we did not understand him at all. We went over the directions a few times to make sure we wouldn't get swallowed up in the prison and never to be heard from again. Another volunteer, his name was Greg, had overheard our clumsy attempt at repeating the directions given by the other volunteer and he offered to take us there. We took him up on his offer and off we went. It wasn't really that hard to find solitary confinement. I can say that now with confidence after all of the years we have been to the prison. We checked the solitary confinement area out and Greg asked us if there was any place else where we wanted to go. We mentioned the guard house, so again, off we went. The guard shack is off the east cell block right on the roof. At midnight the view is really interesting and I highly recommend it if you go for the hunts. While we were on the roof we asked Greg if he has seen anything interesting and where some of the other "hot" spots were. Greg said that he has been a volunteer at the prison for five years and has been in the prison at least 75 times. He said that he has seen the maintenance man many times but the man has been dead for years. Greg also said that he has seen shadows, heard footsteps, and has heard someone calling his name when no one was around. He said that the most interesting places were ones that you couldn't get to. There are some areas that aren't safe to enter and those are some of the areas that have the most activity. They have made great progress in fixing up the prison so we are hoping that sometime in the near future these areas will be accessible to the public who attend these hunts. The last place he took us to was the administration section. This area encompasses three floors and both the ease and west wings. We had just come down the stairs and we were heading to where the wardens office was. I was right behind Greg and the rest of the members with us that night Linda, Dave, Dennis, and Mary were in single file behind us and Brenda was bringing up the rear. We were just about to enter the warden's office when all of a sudden Brenda made a mad dash to the front nearly knocking down the members who were in front of her. Concerned, we asked her what had happened. Brenda said that there was no one behind her since she was the last one in the line. When we came off the stairs she heard footsteps directly behind her.

She thought that maybe some other people that were at the prison attending the hunt was coming up behind her. Brenda looked back to see whom was behind her but there was no one there. She still heard the footsteps but no visible person was making them. That's when she made a beeline for the front of the line.

Something else happened to us during our first time at the prison that hadn't happened to "our" volunteer Greg before. I mentioned above that Greg had been in the prison at least 75 times and he has experienced many things. As he was showing us around the prison one of the places he wanted us to see was the warden's quarters. This consists of numerous rooms on a single floor. There were a couple of bedrooms and a guest room with bath. There is a nice, big, wooden staircase that comes down into the quarter's area, almost right into the heart of the living area. We descended the stairs into the warden's quarters and we all caught a whiff of Lilac perfume. The smell was so strong that it almost hung in the air. Greg told us that he had never smelled that perfume before, especially not in the warden's quarters. Greg also told us that he had either read someplace or someone had told him that the warden's wife liked to wear Lilac perfume all the time. Maybe this was the former warden's long deceased wife, in her own way, letting us know that she was still in the prison after all these years.

The next thing that happened to us was in 2004. It was around 2:30 AM, but before we get to that let's roll the clock back a little so I can tell you the events that led up to it. It was just another investigation at the former prison. Present for this trip were Brenda, James, Dennis, and I. We had gone through the prison a few times and hadn't really seen of felt anything out of the ordinary. Dennis always brings his trailer to the prison. We park it in the parking area. The trailer has beds, AC/heat, a bathroom, kitchen, and power. By this time in the investigation 1-2AM, Brenda was asleep in the bottom bunk in the trailer. Dennis, James, and I went to the "chair room." There wasn't really anything happening here so we decided to continue on to go to the east cell block. Before I continue with the story you are probably wondering what the "chair room" is. I will try to give you the details without being too confusing. The "chair room" is on the third floor, in the administration section of the prison. It is nothing special just a small room off a hallway that has two chairs in it. Rumor has it that if you align the chairs a certain way, then come back later, the chairs will have moved by themselves in the room, so they are not the way that you left them. However, this can't be proven because the room isn't secure and anyone can enter the room and change the chairs around. For example, let's say you arrange the chairs a certain way and then leave. Someone else comes along, because they also have heard of the "chair room," they rearrange the chairs to how they want them, and then they leave. Then you come back and the chairs are not arranged the same way they were when you moved then and then left. As I mentioned earlier we had gone to the chair room and then decided to go to the east cell block. We were in the cell block for approximately 45 minutes and we were taping the whole time with the video camera. We didn't see anything in particular so we planned on leaving the ease cell block and the plan was to go back to the administration section. At this time I stopped recording with the video camera. I would later regret doing so. We exited the cell block on the third floor and entered the administration section. This is where the dive bombing bats come into the picture. We were in some offices when the bats started flying around the room. The bats will actually dive bomb you until you get tired of it and leave the area. When I say dive bombing I literally mean that the bats will fly towards you then they will fly straight at your head then they will pull-up and continue to fly away from you. They will continue doing this until you leave the area. Because we were getting tired us dodging the bats we started to leave the room when two of them came at us at the same time. We ran like the dickens out of the room and down the hall. I wished that I could have had a video camera trained on the hall when we came running by. What happened next was one for the ages. Here were three grown men with their pockets full of equipment running the down the hall trying to outrun these little bats. Dennis had dropped his flashlight while we were running from these bats. Dennis stopped running, and he started to head back the same way we had just came from to pick it up. James told him just leave it behind. James said that we could come back for it later. Dennis stated "It was too expensive; I am getting it back right now!" The whole time this was happening we were all laughing like crazy men. But anyhow we came to a stop at the hall way that runs directly into the chair room. The bats came at us one more time, this time we just ducked, and when I came back up that's when I saw "it." Directly in front of the "chair room," down the hall from us, no more than 20 feet away in clear view was the first and only apparition that I have ever seen. I saw him for around 10-15 seconds and then it was out of sight. It was heading down the hall away from us. At first it didn't register that I just saw a spirit walking the halls. Pretty bad for a ghost hunter huh? I was so unprepared for this that I didn't even get as much as a single picture taken during the time I saw him. I didn't even have the video camera ready as I had just stopped recording after we had left the east cell block. Then I said to the Dennis and James, "Either I just saw a spirit or that was the quietest person you will ever meet because it didn't make a sound as it moved down the hallway." When I saw it there weren't too many people left in the prison and you should have heard footsteps as it went since the floor are tiled and every sound made echoes throughout the halls. Even sounds from another floor can be heard in the prison when everything is quiet. The area where the spirit was heading empties into a hall with three rooms on each side and there is only one way into and out of this area. A few seconds had passed after I had seen the spirit so we decided to chase after the spirit to see if we could find it. James guarded the exit as Dennis and I checked each room, one by one. We didn't find or see anything out of the ordinary. I still can remember what he looked like. The spirit was a male and he had short, light brown / blonde hair and he was wearing dark blue pants and a light blue shirt. I only saw him from the knees up and when he walked his arms were straight at his side and they didn't move. What I did see of his legs didn't move. It was as if he was gliding down the hall. And the thing that I remember the most clearly was what he had around him. He was surrounded entirely by a gold / yellow light. Not like a spot light but it was like I could see his aura, he was surrounded by the light. Being a ghost hunter I wished that I was a little bit more prepared for what I saw and that I was able to remember just a few more details. Having had either the digital camera or camcorder on so I could have maybe captured his image on film would have helped also! But that is the quirks of the field we choose. You have to be prepared for anything, anytime. Nothing else happened during that investigation and to be honest with you nothing could compare to what I had just seen.

Was this the apparition I had seen a few years back at the prison? Did he not have enough energy to show itself so this is the picture I got?

If you ever venture down to the prison I would recommend checking out these places, in no particular order they would be: the warden's quarters, solitary confinement, third floor "hot seat," the basement, west wing showers, and last but certainly not least, the infirmary.

Conclusion-We are not claiming to be the consummate authority figure on hauntings. Just because we think a place is haunted doesn't mean that it is. Just based on the history of the prison and stories from other people that have gone on the ghost hunts over the years you have to think the prison could be haunted. There have been too many prisoners, too many events, and too much emotion not to be. If you get the chance to go down there we highly recommend it. And for what's it worth, you may even see us dragging our equipment around the place trying to find the ever elusive spirit or two. If you see us stop us and say "Hey." And by the way let us know how you like this book. Enjoy your time there and happy hunting.

A-Shopping We Will Go...

Date: 01-05-02
Location: Strip Mall in Chesaning

This investigation fell into our laps. We had a new member, Jeff, tell us about the place. There was a newspaper article about the strip mall and the ghosts that they supposedly had it in. After Jeff had joined the group, his mother sent him the article that appeared in the local newspaper. Jeff asked us if we would be interested in maybe doing an investigation there. We said of course, so Jeff contacted the owners to set up an investigation. When he met the owner, his name is John, he told Jeff that another ghost hunter had stopped by the strip mall and that the person that came out had told him that the ghosts name was "George" and this and that. John wasn't impressed with that person because she didn't have any equipment and just kind of flung her hands in the air saying all kinds of stuff. John wasn't too hot on the idea of having someone else come over to check the place out. Jeff assured him that we were a professional outfit, and that we would be very professional during the investigation. Jeff was able to set up the investigation for early January. The strip mall is like a modern mall, but just a smaller version. You have the main entrance on either end of this long hallway and there are several stores off both sides of the hallway. There is a common area that had bathrooms and a small deli counter where you can get things like pop and chips. Before we get into our investigation let's go over some of the activity that had been reported.

One store that had activity was a candle shop. They have all kinds of candles, all different colors, smells, and shapes. If you like candles you would have a field day in this store. They would leave the shop at night in perfect condition but only to return the next day and find candles on the floor, as if they were being played with like toys.

Another area was a store that had those small figurines. They also had some other knick knacks. Again, when they closed the store for the night all was okay. In the morning when they came to open the store all the figurines would be untouched but the small knick knacks would be scattered all over the floor.

I don't remember where this happened in the mall but one story that was told to us was that a woman saw one of those heavy Santa X-mas decorations float across the room and gently land back on the ground.

We met at a quaint little restaurant a few blocks from the mall. The food was good and the company was better. After we finished our meal we talked about the night's investigation. We then went a few blocks down the street to the strip mall. We had access to the whole mall but since there were different owners for each store, John had to get the other store owners to unlock the door before going into any particular store. We met John and explained how our investigations were conducted.

From our understanding, the property that housed the Strip Mall now was at one time long ago either a lumber mill or carriage house. Either way the property itself has changed over the years.

Before we discuss the investigation results lets cover some of the feelings that we picked up. These feelings are not physical evidence, just feelings the mediums and sensitives picked up.

The first experience that happened to us was in the Basket Barn. There was a couch in the back Jeff picked up on some intense emotional feelings near the couch in the back of the store. Nothing bad just a feeling like something was back there. Jeff was walking near the couch when he became very upset. Jeff said that he felt like there was a child spirit in the store and that she needed help.

Linda also sensed that there was a spirit of a young man in the building. She guessed his age to be in his early 20's, and that he had a problem with his neck. There was a rumor that someone had hung themselves years ago when the place was a lumber mill. Could this be the same person?

The little girl we mentioned in the Basket Barn really gets around the mall. We sensed her spirit near the bathrooms and in the figurine store. The little girl told us, she didn't really speak to us of course, but she communicated to Linda that she likes the figurines in the store but doesn't touch them because she is afraid that she will break them. The little girl likes playing with the candles because she thought they were pretty. The spirit of the little also said that she was killed by a horse and carriage in front of the building. We assume she meant either the lumber yard / carriage house and was brought into the building where she died. She was looking for her mother and wanted to know where she had gone to.

We did have a couple of things happen to us that was quite usual. The first being what happened to us in the card shop. Jeff and I were walking in the card shop and they had these little flags for sale on the front counter. They were just miniature American flags and they were in a coffee cup.

When Jeff and I walked into the store we did notice that the flags were perfectly still, meaning that there was no wind in the store. We walked near the far north end of the store and then made our way to the other end. This time when we passed the flags we noticed that they were fluttering in a slight breeze. We checked the area and couldn't find the source of the breeze. There were no doors open and we could find no source for the breeze. We started to walk away from the flags and we made it just a few feet when something flew at us. I was looking through the video camera's viewfinder and I saw it clearly. Jeff saw it also and asked what that was. I told him I didn't know but I thought I had caught it on camera. It looked like a slim, gray streak of something. I can't really explain how it looked. The thing moved so fast that if you blinked you would miss it. You had to have seen it to know what I mean. When we saw it the thing was arching between us. Like it had been thrown at us from above and it came from the far corner of the store. Still to this day we have no idea what it could have been. And yes we did get it on video but just the last piece of it as it went by us.

The other experience we had was in the store called the "Basket Barn," which was at the far left hand corner of the mall. If you remember previously we did pick up some feelings in this store towards the back. They had a couch that Jeff had a strong, emotional reaction to. We decided to set up a video camera with a tripod just inside the door as well as a motion detector. We figured that if we put the equipment where we did it would essentially cover the whole inside area of the store. Our first indication that something might be amiss in the store happened shortly after we had set up the tripod and video camera and the motion detector was in place. The motion detector started going off but no one was in the area and all of our members were accounted for so they couldn't have been the ones setting off the motion detectors. Sometimes the motion detectors will go off on their own if the batteries are getting bad. We put new batteries in the motion detectors and put it back in the store. Sure enough they started going off again. But when they would go off it was only for a few seconds, then they would stop making noise. If the batteries were the issue it will continue to go off until you turn it off. So we knew the batteries were not the issue.

We thought maybe it was a defective unit, but it had worked fine the previous investigation that we did. We decided to stay in the store, out of range of the motion detectors, to see if anything would be visible to the naked eye. Again the motion detectors went off but we could see nothing that might be triggering the motion detectors. Someone suggested that the members in the store were now setting it off. So we moved towards the back of the store, we should have been totally out of its range now. Again it started going off. This time we showed everyone that we were not the ones setting it off. We looked like crazy people because we were jumping up and down, swinging our arms, trying to make it go off. We couldn't make the motion detectors go off. From where we were standing there was no way that we were causing the motion detector to go off. This continued for around 1 hour. The motion detectors would sound the alarm and then go silent. Sound the alarm and then go silent. They just kept on with this cycle the whole hour. We checked the video after the investigation but we didn't get anything on video. This might have been caused by the camera being too high or too low. The video camera covers only so much area and it is possible that whatever the thing was that was causing the motion detector to go off was not in the view of the camera.

I just thought of another thing that happened to us during the investigation. There were three of us standing next to a small table in the main hallway. We were taking the equipment from the cases and putting them on the table. We were all a few feet from the table when one of the EMF meters we had placed on the table just a few moments earlier flew off. It didn't just fall over and we were all far enough from the table that one of us didn't accidently bump the table and cause it to fall over. The EMF meter flew off the table and landed a few feet away. We all just stood there, too stunned to say anything. Was there a spirit or two present and were just saying "hi"?

These were the three things that happened to us during the investigation that night. It was a good investigation and we hope to go back there again.

Conclusion-From the stories that were told to us from the employees and the activity that happened to us we would tend to believe that the Market Square Mall is haunted. We made contact with at least two spirits and there could be more there. This mall is a nice place to shop. If you are ever in the area, stop in and say "hi."

Gettysburg...

Date: Numerous trips
Location: Gettysburg, PA

Gettysburg is one of our favorite places to visit. We have gone there every year for the last 5 years. We just can't seem to get enough of the town. I would recommend the trip to anyone that has an interest not only in the paranormal, but in history also. The town itself is a small, quaint little town. I don't know the population but it can't be more that 10,000 people, if even that many.

During the civil war there was a great battle that took place during July 1-3 in 1863. During that time, the population of Gettysburg was only 2400 people. The armies of the Confederate states and the Army of the Potomac converged here and for 3 days a battle raged. There were over 50,000 casualties suffered on both sides. There was no area spared from the fighting. There were skirmishes to the North, South, East, and West. During the first day when the Union Army retreated back to Cemetery Ridge, the Confederate army chased them through town, killing some but taking many more prisoners. One civilian, a woman named Jennie Wade, was killed during the battle. She was killed by a stray bullet while in her sister's kitchen baking bread for the Union soldiers.

I read somewhere that Gettysburg is considered the most haunted battlefield in America. You will get no arguments from me. There have been many documented reports of people hearing, seeing, and smelling things that cannot be logically explained.

Some of the more common places that have had reported activity have names like; Devil's Den, the Wheatfield, Little Round Top, Peach Orchid, and The Angle. Now these places represent only a small fraction of the places in Gettysburg that are haunted. But think about this for a moment. There was a lot of misery, suffering and death that took place on this battlefield and surrounding areas. There are many places that you might be able to get activity. Just have respect for the area and what happened there.

Before I tell you what we have experienced while in Gettysburg let me relate a couple of the better known occurrences that have happened there.

The first one happened during the filming of the epic movie "Gettysburg." This movie was from the early 1990's I believe and there were many re-enactors, many in period dress in town for the movie as they served as extra's during the battle scenes. During any given day there are usually a handful of re-enactors on the streets of Gettysburg. Sometimes to be honest you don't know if they are real or if they are spirits and they might just vanish before your eyes. Anyway, let's get back to the story. Some of the townspeople volunteered to shuttle the re-enactors from where the filming was taking place back to their hotels in town. This one woman had a pickup truck and she was bringing 3 re-enactors back into town after a day of filming. She said that she dropped them off at the hotel and went back out to pick up some more people. After a few minutes she looked in her rearview mirror and saw someone in period dress sitting in the bed of the truck. She thought that someone was trying to scare her so she pulled over and got out of her truck to confront the person she had seen. When she looked in the bed of the truck there was no one there. It was totally empty of any living beings. There was no way that someone could have jumped out when she was driving and she didn't see anyone get out after she had stopped. She chalked it up to one of the spirits long since deceased was just hitching a ride back to the battlefield. They say that people in period dress will actually attract the spirits because the spirits of the soldiers that died in the battle will be drawn to the re-enactors because they are dressed the way the soldiers would have been if you were here for the battle. I think that the saying goes something like this "Things that are similar attract" applies here. Maybe after all these years the spirits feel "safe" with people that are dressed like them. Maybe there is some kind of comfort level that is being played out here.

The other more famous sighting happened sometime in the 1980's and I apologize for not knowing the exact date but I think it was in 1983. From what I understand there were VIP's from Russia and they were seeing America for the first time. So the United States arranged for them to see some famous sites and the Gettysburg Military Park was one of those places they were to visit. The park service controls the Military Park so they set the hours, what you can and cannot see, and they strictly regulate which group of re-enactors can use the park for their drilling. Anyway, these VIP's were riding around the park in a car when they saw some soldiers drilling in an open field. They all got out of the car to watch these men as they drilled. They were very impressed with the soldiers and thanked the park ranger for having the event planned just for them. The park ranger told them that there were no soldiers on the fields that day and that the park service didn't plan this for them. What they saw were some soldiers long since deceased who were still on the field heading for a battle that was waged over 150 years ago.

Now let me relate some of our stories during our many stays in Gettysburg. During our first visit there we stayed at the Cashtown Inn which is an historic building that has been turned into a Bed and Breakfast. The Inn is 8 miles west of Gettysburg on US-30. As the legend goes, long ago there were 2 wagons passing each other, one coming into town and the other one leaving. The one driver of one of the wagons leaving the town told the other driver coming into town to make sure that he had cash with him because the next town was Cashtown. He said this because the owner of the Inn in the town would only accept cash for a room and no bartering was allowed. Hence the name has stuck over the years. During the Gettysburg campaign some of the Confederate army passed right in front of the hotel. I also heard that some of the Confederate generals stayed there briefly. If you ever watch the movie "Gettysburg," make sure that you watch for the scene that has the Cashtown Inn prominently displayed in the scene.

We arrived at the Inn early so we were the only guests that had checked in, even though the Inn was full for the night. The owner's son, Rod, was there and he showed us to our room. We were standing in the hallway at our door when we asked Rod about the Inn and the rumors that it was haunted. He said that he didn't mention it to people unless they asked first. It seems that some people are afraid to sleep in a haunted place, go figure. Anyway, he told us some stories of guests that had seen things, heard things, and have taken pictures in the hotel and have gotten orbs and other things on film. As we were talking we all heard voices coming from the room across the hall from us. It sounded like 2 men were having a conversation. Rod looked at us and told us that all the rooms should be empty and that there shouldn't be anyone in the room since we were the first ones to check in. We went over to the room and Rod knocked on the door. As soon as he did the talking in the room abruptly stopped. He announced himself and used his master key to enter the room. It was empty and there was no one in the bathroom. All three of us heard the voices clearly. Just another example of an unexplained event that can happen in and around the town of Gettysburg.

We were staying at the Cashtown Inn just for the week-end but the room we stayed in on Friday was not available for Saturday. We had to move across the hall to a different room Saturday night. The first room we stayed at was the famous room 4. Each room has journals so if you stay in the room and if you experience anything not "normal," you can write down anything that you experienced during your stay and the next person that stays in the room can read about what other people have experienced. This seems like a good idea but on the other hand, the power of suggestion can be powerful. It seems that the Inn has a few resident spirits still here after all these years. It was reported in the journal for room 4 that someone would knock on the door early in the morning. When the occupants of the room would get out of bed and open the door, no one was there. From what we read in the journal the time varied between 2-4 AM. We didn't experience anything that night but after driving for over 10 ½ hours, then spending the night in town and getting back late, maybe we were so tired and slept so soundly that nothing, not even a spirit or two, could have woken us up that night. The night in the other room was just as quiet. I did have a hard time sleeping and sometime during the early morning I thought I smelled the aroma of tobacco. I might have been imagining things, but I am sure that I could smell it in the air. On day 2 in Gettysburg we met up with Dave and Linda, members and friends, they stayed in Gettysburg at a quaint B&B next to the Dobbins House. We did the usual shopping and things until around 8PM. The park closes at 10PM SHARP. The park rangers will give you a ticket if you stay out after closing. I can attest to this personally.

We hit all the usual spots that are reputed to be haunted. This was our first time there and we didn't know of the spots that we know about now. We took pictures and got the usual orbs in them. We did find a cold spot on Little Round Top and have this picture with a bright orb. At exactly 9:45 PM we took Dave and Linda back to their place, which was right across the street from the National Cemetery. We had a couple of EMF meters with us and Dave was holding the one that would give you an audible beep if the EMF field had changed. We were right in front of National Cemetery, one block from their place, when we started hearing this beeping sound. Our first thought was that something was wrong with the car. But this wasn't the case. Dave looked down and the EMF meter he was holding was going off. This only happens when the meter detects a change in the EMF field, which spirits are suspected of altering. This will in turn cause the EMF meter to sound an alarm. So this meant that either the meter was going off because of the cemetery or something was in the car with us. We pulled into their driveway and got out of the car. I immediately took some pictures. In one picture there were 3 orbs around us and then I took a picture across the street towards National Cemetery. Right there, in the center of the picture, was the brightest and biggest orb I have ever seen in my life. This orb was huge and was moving pretty fast since there was a rather large tail behind it. To this day I don't know if we had someone hitching a ride that night or if they came from the cemetery. Either way, it was an experience that was really interesting.

An orb in Gettysburg, Pa right across the street from the National Cemetery. Who was this and why is it moving so fast?

We have been there many times since that first time. The other times we have gone to Gettysburg the children have been with us so we couldn't really go out and do some hunting. Like I said before, if you have the chance to go to Gettysburg by all means go. Even if "ghosts" are not your cup of tea, there are many shops and things to do that don't require sneaking around in the dark. But it is really fun to be on Little Round Top and look down at Devil's Den at night and see all the flashes going off from fellow hunters taking pictures, trying to capture the elusive ghost at Gettysburg.

Conclusion-They don't call Gettysburg the most haunted piece of land in America for nothing. The local business's all carry assorted books on Gettysburg haunts. The local B&B's have some sort of ghost events scheduled at their place of business. Many brave men died during the battle of Gettysburg. It seems like they have never left the hallowed grounds. There have been many stories, events, sights and sounds to suggest that there is something paranormal happening here. Why don't you come to Gettysburg and see for yourself.

Wine with Our Meal?

Date: 10-26-05
Location: Fenton Hotel

We have wanted to investigate the Fenton Hotel for many years. The hotel is no longer a hotel but they offer fine dining on the main floor. But for some reason or another neither the hotels nor our schedules would give us a mutual date. Because of this we never have been able to investigate this hotel. All of this changed in October of 2005 when we were contacted by WEYI-TV 25 from Flint. They were interested in doing a spot about us and whether we knew of a place where we could do an investigation. We contacted Nick, the owner of the Fenton Hotel, and asked him if we could bring the TV crew with us and conduct an investigation. The segment was going to air during the week of Halloween. Nick graciously allowed us to do this. Nick and his staff were really nice people and we felt welcomed in the hotel.

There have been many articles written about the hotel and its spirits. One of the better ones involves a man who orders a drink and a waitress that came to his table. It seems that one night, and this has happened many times since, a waitress had a gentlemen sitting at her table. She went over to him and asked him what she could get for him. He ordered his drink, which was usually a Jack and coke, and the waitress went to the bar and poured his drink. When she came back to the table with his drink, he was gone. Now it is entirely possible that the man was flesh and blood, and he just walked off without waiting for his drink. But it is also totally feasible that he was a spirit and just vanished. He has been seen numerous times and always at the same table. So I think we can say with some certainty that the gentleman in question is a spirit at the hotel and that he still enjoys his drinks.

The only date that we could do the investigation was on a Tuesday. The news crew was on a deadline and this was the one and only day they could do it. We normally do investigations on weekends, because like most of us, we work and after working the whole day, plus travel time, we don't feel like doing an investigation. But in this case we made an exception and made arrangements with Nick to come out on Tuesday and conduct the investigation.

As it turned out we were the first ones from the team that had arrived at the hotel so we took it upon ourselves to seek Nick out and introduce ourselves to him. Nick is a really nice person. Nick said that we could go anywhere in the hotel that we wanted to go but the third floor, which is no longer in use but once housed the rooms in the hotel. Nick said that the door to the third floor was nailed shut but said that if we wanted to go up there he would open the door for us. The news crew arrived as we were talking to Nick and they introduced themselves to him also. Nick also told us that the TV crew could film anywhere in the hotel, even interviewing staff and customers if they wanted to.

The rest of the team arrived and we went on a quick tour of the hotel. When you first come into the hotel, you are standing in a reception area, I don't know the proper name, but it is where you wait for the hostess to seat you. The restaurant is usually pretty busy and there is usually a wait to be seated. The interior of the hotel is reminiscent of the grand hotels from long ago. Nice artwork, wood crafting, and fine fixtures make this a hotel that you must see at least once. Off to your right are tables and if you walk a few feet straight ahead, to your left are stairs that will lead you to the second floor. If you continue straight ahead and veer a little to your left, there is a long bar with stools on your right. Here you can have a few cold ones while watching sports on TV. At the end of the bar and to your right is the kitchen. Straight ahead and to your right, near the far corner of the room, is the table that the mysterious gentleman orders his drink then disappears.

If you go back to the stairs that go to the second floor and go up, you come to a hallway. To your left is a ballroom that was once used for dancing. If you turn right and continue down the hall there is one room on each side. If you turn around and head back to the stairs, you will see the door that leads you up to the third floor. Nick wasn't kidding, the door is nailed shut.

Once the door was opened we did venture up to the third floor. It hadn't been used in years. You could just imagine the place in its heyday. The rooms were pretty good size and there were even a few suites up there. Linda and I were getting a few names of the spirits up there. We also felt that someone had lost a baby up there and that she was trying to find it.

We decided to set up the equipment in the hall up on the second floor. Something of interest happened while we were bringing up the equipment from the parking lot. Jeff, Holly, Linda, and I were the only ones up on the second floor. Holly and Linda were near the stairs and Jeff and I were near the rooms. We all heard a woman's voice and she said "Help." We all looked at each other simultaneously and almost in unison we asked if we had heard the voice. We all said that yes, we heard it. What a way to start an investigation. We had our full compliment of equipment so we set up a video camera and a motion detector at the end of the hall, near the rooms. We also set the Trifield EMF meter there also. James set his camera in the ballroom and he did get some good orbs on video. The other camera was placed on the top of the stairs looking down. So if anything was trying to get up or down the stairs we would see it.

We decided to put the wireless camera in the room with the table where the man orders the drink. We figured that this would be a good time to try and catch him there.

So like all of our investigations, we set up all the video monitors and watched for any activity on them. Occasionally, one or two of the members would grab a piece of equipment and walk around. But generally we just sit and watch the video monitors and see what transpires. The TV crew was walking around, getting the interview part done. They then came up to the second floor and filmed us with the equipment. Our members who were willing to be interviewed had their time in front of the TV camera, answering questions from Kelly and we also explained the our equipment to the TV crew and what each one was used for.

It was during this point that we found that we had something unexpected on video. The TV crew asked us if we had found anything so far because they wanted to use it for the segment they were doing. During our investigation we did notice an unexplained shadow that appeared on the wall near the stairs. We thought this shadow would be a great part of the TV segment so were trying to find that on the video cameras when we found something totally by accident. Holly had stopped the tape right before the shadow and when she played the tape back you could hear what sounded like a baby crying. It was a very clear and definite sound. What was funny was that Linda and I both felt that a spirit on the third flood had lost a baby and was trying to find it. We played it again and the TV crew recorded it.

That's when Kelly, the reporter for the TV station, told us that when she was interviewing the hostess downstairs, the hostess mentioned that the manager heard a baby crying on the second floor one night. When they went up to investigate there was nothing to be found. Whether or not the sound we got was the same baby sound that was heard that night, we will never probably know for sure.

What are the chances of having the same sound heard by different people in a hotel this size and not be the same sound?

Just to show how hospitable Nick was, some members ordered food from the menu because since it was a week-day investigation some members didn't have time to eat before the investigation. Nick let us order things from the menu at no charge. I thought that was worth mentioning here, and we wish to thank Nick again for the meals.

The investigation was coming to an end as it was getting close to the closing time for the hotel. We started to pick up the equipment that we had scattered all over the hotel. We gathered up all the cases and started the trek from the second floor of the hotel to our cars in the parking lot. I like to joke with people and tell them that once we show up for an investigation we literally take over the place, this was no exception. We said our goodbye to Nick and he offered to buy us a drink at the bar. We accepted, but it was pop, and sat down for a few minutes. When we were finished we thanked Nick again and left. The TV crew was still in the parking lot. They were filming exterior shots before they left. We exchanged business cards and we went home.

Conclusion- Is the Fenton Hotel haunted. I would have to give a resounding yes! From the data that we gathered to the baby sound we recorded, to the impressions that we were getting upstairs, there is definitely some spirits still hanging around the place. Whether or not this hotel was their old stomping ground is hard to say but they are still here for some reason. We were in touch with Kelly from the TV station after the piece aired and she told me that they received a lot of positive comments of the show and that some people wanted more. She said that some people told her that the baby crying part gave them shivers and some wanted the piece to be longer.

Food and Spirits...

Date: Numerous
Location: Linden Hotel

We were contacted by a newspaper reporter from Fenton, her name was Laurie, to possibly do an investigation at the Linden Hotel and she would tag along and then write an article for her paper. She already had talked to the owner of the Hotel and he gave his approval to do an investigation. We asked her some of the things that had been reported by the workers and customers. Laurie said that many people heard footsteps, doors opening and closing, and some were hearing their names being called. This sounded intriguing so we set up a date and time to do the investigation.

Like the Fenton Hotel the Linden Hotel is no longer a hotel. They have turned the upstairs, where the rooms used to be, into a sports bar. There is family dining on the first floor. We arrived a little early and met the owner, Jack, and his daughter Susan. Jack is a nice guy. He gave us free run of the place. We have been back a few times and he and his staff have always been really nice to us.

There are two doors to the hotel, actually there are three, but the last one isn't used. There is the side door which takes you to the sports bar upstairs and there is a main door, the one that we used, which opens into the main dining area. There is a jukebox to your right and the rest is for dining. There is a bar right in front of you as you walk in. Again you can have a cold one while watching TV. If you turn left and walk a few feet you will see the stairs that takes you

148

upstairs. While upstairs, at the far end on your left is another bar area. It is worth mentioning that there is a small room just past the bar. This is used by the DJ to store his CD's, stereo, and speakers. There are also a few TV's up here. At the far end of the room are the stairs that take you to the kitchen.

The only bad thing about this investigation was that the hotel was still open. There were customers coming and going as well as talking and smoking. We couldn't really set up anything like the video cameras, motion detectors, or the Trifield EMF. We could have but we would have gotten pictures of people moving around and they would in turn set off the motion detectors. We decided that we would just walk around taking pictures with the digital camera and using the other EMF meters that we have. We took the equipment that we could and fanned out in the hotel. Some places in the hotel were more "active" than others, so we focused on these areas because of the activity that was reported in these areas.

Even without us being able to use most of the equipment we did have a couple of things of interest happen to us.

The first one involved Jack's daughter Susan, who was working behind the bar upstairs during this investigation. Another member and I were walking just in front of the bar. I was holding one of our EMF meters and just as I got to the corner of the bar I started to get high EMF readings. High EMF readings can be caused by man-made objects like TV's, outlets, and fans. We always take base readings before the investigation starts and there were no high EMF readings in the area where I was now picking them up. We checked the area for high EMF readings and as soon as we strayed from where the readings were high they would go back to normal. When we went to the same corner of the bar the EMF readings went high again. I commented to Susan that the EMF readings were really high and we started to take some pictures of the area. Susan grabbed a glass to serve a drink and the glass totally shattered in her hands. I am not talking about breaking apart into 2 or 3 big pieces, this glass literally exploded into a million pieces. I would not have believed it had I not been right there, no more than 5 feet away and saw the whole thing. We made sure that she was okay. She was understandably a little upset but otherwise she was fine and we made note of it on our log.

The other thing that happened involved the ladies bathroom. Back when the hotel was an actual working hotel, there were guest rooms where the restrooms are now. The bathrooms, both the ladies and men's, are side by side. There has been reported paranormal activity in both of the restrooms. The activity has ranged from hearing their names called while using the rest rooms to having the door open and close by its self. We always put our cases of equipment on the table's right next to the bathrooms during our investigations. We were just sitting there talking when Brenda asked if there was anyone in the ladies restroom. We said that we didn't think so and why was she asking. She said that she saw a shadow under the door, like someone was there. Brenda and a few lady members went in there and nope, there was not a living soul in there. Brenda snapped a few pictures and in one there was a bright orb.

The last thing that happened was with our old digital camera. This thing didn't even have a flash and the pixels were something like 640x240, the thing wasn't even a mega pixel. Needless to say the pictures taken were not very crisp or clear. Brenda was taking pictures and she took a picture of a Red Wings poster that was on the wall. This was the year that they won the Stanley Cup and everything that had the Red Wings on it was popular. After she took the picture we downloaded it to the laptop. The poster wasn't even in the picture, instead there was something that I can't explain and haven't seen anything like it since. The best way to describe it is to say that there were things that you can't even begin to describe. But one thing that you could make out was a little girl with blonde hair wearing a nightgown. She was barefoot and standing on her tippy toes. Here is just a little more information about this picture. After subsequent visits to the hotel we have learned that a little girl had indeed died in one of the hotel rooms. There was a fire that was caused by a wood burning stove and she didn't make it out alive

It was nearing the time that they had karaoke so we decided it was a good time to leave. We packed up what equipment we had used, we did this to the sounds of "Ghostbusters" blaring from the DJ's speakers. Karaoke night at the Linden Hotel had now begun. We found Jack and thanked him again. Jack said that we were welcome back anytime. We told him that we would take him up on his offer sometime.

We have been back to the hotel a few more times, but we never have had the experiences that we did that first time. We have been back there with both TV crews from WJRT-TV 12 and WSMH-66 both of them from Flint. Not at the same time mind you but at different times. You would think that the spirits would want to be on TV and cause some mischief. But then again, maybe they were camera shy or if you think about it, maybe TV didn't even exist when they were alive and they have no idea what in the heck all the cameras and lights are.

Jack told us some stories of things that have been going on at the hotel in years past. One I thought was the best. Jack said that one night after closing he was eating a burger in the sports bar watching TV before heading home. The door to the men's bathroom squeaks really loud when opened. If you hear it, you would know what it was, especially in an empty and quiet hotel. He was alone upstairs when he heard the door to the men's room open and close. He had heard it before so it didn't bother him. He said that after a few minutes, it opened again and this time he heard footsteps. Not wanting to tempt fate Jack said that he got up, turned off the TV and went home. He said that most things that happen in the hotel don't bother him, but for some reason that time it did.

Actually, one story just came to mind that Jack told us the last time that we were there. It seems that a family, which consisted of a mom, dad, and a daughter, came to the hotel to eat dinner one night. When the family left the hotel they noticed their daughter was talking to someone in the back seat of the car. They didn't think much of it until they got home that night. Everyone had gone to bed and the mom was doing what mom's do, checking the doors and windows before going to bed. She happened to look outside at the pool and noticed there was a little girl standing there. The moms first thought was what was a girl that little doing out at this time and if she wasn't careful she might fall into the pool. She went to open the patio door to go outside and the little girl was gone. She said that she had on a white nightgown and had light blonde hair. The next night the mom saw the little girl again. The mom again started to go outside to confront the girl, but again she just vanished. The mom hasn't seen the little girl since. The next day the mom asked their daughter who she was talking to in the car the night coming back from the hotel. The daughter said she talking to a little girl that followed them from the hotel and that she followed them home from the hotel. So is it possible that the girl from the hotel followed the girl home? Yes it is possible. Did it happen, hard to say? But children and pets can see things that we can't. So I would tend to believe that it did happen.

Conclusion- The original location for the hotel was actually a few blocks away from its present location. It was moved some years ago. The hotel was in operation as far back as the 1800's, if my memory serves me correctly. There have been many, many people that have gone in and out of her doors. There would be a range of emotions carried into this building and some of it may have been trapped here. From the investigations that we have done in the past to all the reports from workers and customers alike, we believe that the hotel is haunted.

The Owner Is Still Here...

Date: 10-07-04
Location: Holly Hotel

We had done a newspaper interview with a reporter from Oakland County; his name is Gary, a few years before. Gary covered our Pontiac investigation that we had done a few years earlier. Gary made contact with us asking if we would be interested in doing an investigation at the Holly Hotel. He would of course follow us during the investigation and write an article to appear in his paper. To be honest with you we hadn't even heard of the Holly Hotel until he mentioned it. We told him that he would have to get back with him. Gary e-mailed us a few days later and that he had talked with the owner of the Holly Hotel and that everything was a go. He suggested a date that both the hotel owner and he had open on their schedules. There was a slight problem with the date chosen. We had an investigation at a home in Garden City on the same day that he proposed doing the hotel. We asked him if we could investigate the hotel at 11 PM on that day. That would give us enough time to investigate the Garden City home, then make the trek north to Holly and conduct the investigation there at the hotel. Gary told us he would contact the owner and he would get back to us. Gary sent us an e-mail a few days later and said that everything was set and that he would meet us at the hotel around 10:45 PM. We agreed to this and told him we would see him then.

The day started out in Garden City, which is a suburb of Detroit. The investigation there ended at 9 PM. We then packed up the van and headed north to Holly. We got to the city of Holly at 10:30 PM. We found a parking spot across the street and made our way to the hotel.

Like her predecessors in the previous hotel investigations, the Holly Hotel is no longer a working hotel. The first and second floors are dining facilities and the third floor is the attic. She still has the same old grander that made her one of the finer hotels in her heyday. If you close your eyes you can imagine the people that once stayed and ate in this fine hotel. There is I am sure a lot of history in this hotel. I was told that there was once a train station across the street and that the Holly Hotel once was a popular spot for out of town travelers to spend the night before continuing on their journey.

When you enter the front door, you are in a rather large area that looked like the front desk of a hotel. There is a large wooden counter and behind it what looked like places where they would put messages in if you were staying in one of the rooms. They are often referred to as pigeon holes. If you went through the door way on your right, there is a large dining area. The door way to your left took you to the bar and some table and chairs for sitting. If you continue straight, to your right are the stairs that led you up to the second floor. In front of you, just past the stairs, was a stroke of genius. They had private dining rooms that looked like old train cars. They even had the overhead compartments that was stocked full of old luggage. You felt like you were on an old dining car from the old days. I would have loved to be alive during the "good old days" and take train rides where you could eat and sleep on the trains.

If you took the stairs to the second floor, you came out right near the bathrooms. The bathrooms, like the ones at the Linden Hotel, seemed to be some of the more active places in the hotel. If you turned right and went 50 feet, there was a door that opened to the upstairs kitchen. Immediately to you right was another dining area. If you went back to where we came up the stairs, straight ahead was the liquor storage area. This room actually had a padlock on the outside. To your left was another dining area. This one had a small bar in it just as you walked in, and to your left. If you took the stairs to the third floor you were in a massive attic. The whole floor was storage space.

When we arrived, the owner, Christine, was unavailable but we were told by the hotel workers she would be with us soon. Everyone from the group was already there so we decided to go to the bar and have a few drinks and wait. Yes, we had pop again. Gary from the paper came in and we all sat and waited for Christine. She arrived a few minutes later and gave us a tour of the hotel. Christine told us that we could go anywhere in the hotel that we wanted. Christine also told us some of the "ghost" stories that have occurred in the hotel, here are a few of them.

It seems that the previous owner used to smoke cigars. As we came in the front door we noticed that there was a big old chair near the door. That was his chair and they put it near the door as a spot of honor. It seems that the old gentleman never left. He has been spotted at various places in the hotel and many people have smelled cigar smoke near his chair. They only get a quick smell of cigar smoke, and then the aroma is gone.

Another story is about a place that could very well be the most haunted location in the hotel, the men's restroom. It seems that more than one gentleman, while in the restroom, has encountered the "nice looking woman." The story I was told happened just a few days before our investigation. It seems that a man was in one of the stall in the restroom. As he was sitting there he heard the door open to the bathroom. No big deal since it is a public restroom. But he didn't see or hear anybody come into the restroom. He thought that someone just changed their mind about coming in and he didn't think anything more of it. After he was finished, the man was at the sink washing his hands. He happened to look in the mirror and behind him was a pretty young woman. He was shocked to (1.) See a woman in the men's bathroom with him and (2.) He didn't see her come in. The man turned to face the woman and he said that the woman said something to him that he couldn't understand and she just vanished. He said that she was standing right in front of him one minute and gone the next.

After we were given the grand tour by Christine we decided that the second floor would be a perfect place to take over as our staging area and open the cases of equipment that we have. We said our opening prayer and some members grabbed the EMF meters, one took the tape recorder to try and get some EVP, and Brenda took the digital camera and everyone basically went in all directions. They had places they wanted to check out and off they went.

We decided to set up one video camera up stairs in the attic. There was really no reason other than the fact that we have heard stories about the third floor and decided that we would give it a try. We set up another video camera in the second floor hallway, right in front of the men's room. We wanted to see if any spirit, male or female, would either enter or exit the restroom. If any spirit made an appearance, we would be there to capture it on video. Then, believe it or not, we even put a video camera in the men's room. We wanted to make sure all possible areas were covered. We usually are not this weird to have video camera's inside the men's room but in this case with all the stories about the room, we couldn't resist. And yes, we did notify everyone that entered the men's room that there was a video camera in the room and it was recording.

We walked around the hotel and at one point there were 4 of us standing by the previous owners chair near the front door when there was an unmistakable odor of cigar smoke. My grandpa used to smoke cigars and the smell was very similar to his. We all confirmed that we smelled this and we started taking pictures. Out of all the pictures that we took at that moment only a couple had orbs in them.

This orb was captured at the Holly Hotel. Is this a long since deceased customer returning for a meal?

That was the only activity that we had that night. We got some orbs with the digital camera, but very little else in terms of evidence. It just was a quiet night. This proves that just because a place might have activity doesn't mean you will always get any evidence on either your camera or video camera.

We decided to pack things up early due to the fact that we had done an investigation earlier in the day. We thanked Christine for allowing us in and that we would be in touch. We then went upstairs and packed up the equipment and took them down to the van. We said our closing prayer and then left to go home.

Charles sent me an e-mail saying that he might have gotten something on video at the hotel. He wanted me to see it so he sent me a copy via e-mail. What Charles got, in my opinion, was an apparition on video. To have this is very rare and we believe Charles captured one a video. The video was taken with his video camera on the second floor. It was when we were packing up the equipment. Charles had the video camera facing one of the dining rooms upstairs. In the video you see an employee of the hotel carrying a chair to the storage room when she walks right in front of and then passes the camera. When she passes the video camera something comes out of the dining room, reacts like oops they are still here, and then ducks back into the dining room. No one with us that night was wearing what this person in the video was wearing. I don't know who or what was on the video that Charles got. I can safely say that it wasn't anyone of us. Maybe a spirit was trying to make itself known to us after all.

Conclusion- Is the Holly Hotel haunted? Before we went there to do an investigation we had heard stories about the place. We had read some of the personal accounts. Based on what we experienced I would have to say that yes, the place has a spirit or two roaming around. Having been at the front door and smelled the cigar smoke when no one was smoking helped to convince us. When Charles sent me the video with the apparent apparition in the upstairs dining room that sealed the deal for me. We have wanted to go back to the hotel again, but for whatever reason we haven't been able to go, at least not yet.

Who's There...?

Date: October 13th, 1997
Location: Cemetery in Gratiot County

This next investigation is a flashback to the good old days when the only place that we could do an investigation was a cemetery. This investigation is old school for us and I thought I would include it for all you out there that like a good cemetery as well as we do.

The cemetery we did an investigation at was nothing special. No family members were buried there, no friends either. The place wasn't even known to be haunted. Back then we were just ghost hunters that didn't have a clue what to do or how to conduct a proper investigation. We have come a long ways since then. Hope you enjoy the story.

The cemetery in question is only a few miles from my mom's house. We picked up my cousin Marc at his house, dropped the kids off at grandma's, and headed to the cemetery. I know a few people that are buried there but they were just neighbors that had passed away over the years. This was so early in the days of SEMGHS that we didn't have any equipment. I had just a regular 35MM camera, and an RCA video camera with no external lights and a tripod. Marc had a video camera that didn't have a light either and was basically useless after dark just like mine was. We had a Ford Bronco at the time and Brenda sat in the front seat most of the time. She wasn't into the ghost hunting back then, just went along to humor me I think. We had parked near a small mausoleum that was at the south east corner of the cemetery. Like I said before, Brenda stayed in the Bronco and Marc and I went out into the cemetery. We were just walking around and seeing if we could feel anything. At one tombstone we could feel a cold spot. Since we didn't have any equipment we couldn't tell how much of a change it was. But you could definitely feel the coldness. We took some pictures and after we got them back from being processed, we didn't have a digital camera back then, there was some Ectoplasmic mist in the same area that we felt the cold spot.

Marc said that he was going to sit down for awhile and just see if anything would come to him so he could get it on video. I told Marc that while he was sitting down I was going to go into the mausoleum and see if there was anything in there. I walked over to the mausoleum, walked in, and closed the door. I placed the video camera on the tripod and placed it just inside the front door. I had the video camera facing the opposite end of the mausoleum and turned it on and started recording. I never knew that a place could be this dark. It was kind of cool because there were things that looked like sky lights in this building. I guess they wanted who ever was interred here to have some natural light. Anyway, the moon in conjunction with the skylights made the room hazy with a blue/white light. Considering I was in a place with dead people I could have gotten used to this. I thought that since I was there I might take some pictures. I asked if there was anyone present with me if I could take their picture. I took a couple of pictures at random. I decided that I was going to walk to the far end of the mausoleum and see what I could find there and maybe take a few pictures. The place had a tile floor so when you walked your shoes made a squeaking like noise. As you walked it was like squeak, squeak, until you stopped walking. As I walked you could hear the squeaking of my shoes. I was just a few feet from the wall at the other end when I stopped walking, squeak, squeak, squeak, and then nothing. Hey wait a minute. I stopped walking but I am still hearing footsteps behind me.

There were three extra steps after I stopped walking. Now for the big question, who or what was behind me? I turned so fast that if anything was behind me I would have caught them so off guard they wouldn't have time to react fast enough. But there was nothing behind me, at least nothing that I could see. I was alone in this building, or so I thought. So I fired off a few shots with the camera hoping to catch something. When I got the pictures back there were two bright orbs in the building with me.

I thought maybe there were loose tiles or something that might cause the extra "steps" that I heard. I walked towards the front of the mausoleum to test this theory. As I walked my shoes squeaked, as I knew they would. When I stopped at the front of the building the sound stopped, there were no extra footsteps this time. Okay, there was nothing following me this time. Now to really test my theory about the loose tiles I would walk towards the back of the mausoleum again. I went the same way again towards the back. I wanted to see if the floor caused the sounds I heard before. As I expected there was the same squeaking sound as I walked. As I got closer to the back wall I stopped and eagerly listened. Nothing but quiet. This time there was no extra sounds. I was in the same place near the wall as before. The only difference was that this time when I stopped there was no extra noise. There was nothing walking behind me this time. I then walked towards the front door, but this time I was leaving the building. I thanked whatever was in there with me and took a couple of parting shots with the camera. I grabbed the video camera and tripod and turned off the video camera. I then proceeded out the door and closed it behind me.

I went to where I left Marc and sure enough he was still there resting in the same spot, he hadn't moved an inch. It was getting late but we decided to make one last sweep of the cemetery before we left. Wondering where Brenda was? She was still sitting in the front seat of the Bronco.

Marc and I went to the farthest corner of the cemetery away from Brenda and the Bronco. We finished up the film in the camera so we headed back to the Bronco to reload and go back out into the cemetery. Brenda opened up the door and said that we have to leave right now. I told her that we weren't finished yet and that we were going back out. She insisted that we leave right now. I mumbled something under my breath then Marc and I packed up the camera and video camera, we hopped into the Bronco, with Brenda, and we left for town. We dropped Marc off at his house and we went to pick up the kids at grandmas.

On the way home she told me why she wanted to leave so fast from the cemetery. We were there in October so the trees had lost most of their leaves and the leaves were on the ground. When the leaves start drying out, whenever someone walks on them they crunch under your feet. Brenda said that Marc and I were in the cemetery taking pictures. We were in clear view of her of the whole time. She then heard the leaves rustling behind the truck. She said that it sounded like someone was walking up behind the truck. She wanted no part of this and didn't care to see what or who was back there. Brenda said that when Marc and I started walking back to the truck to change film in the camera, the rustling noise stopped. That's why she was so insistent on leaving and that meant right now.

Conclusion- We definitely experienced more than we bargained for in the cemetery. It was just supposed to be a nice quiet ghost hunt and it turned out to be a pretty active night. We will say that the cemetery does have some kind of activity in it.

Discovery Channel Experience...

This section is about our appearance on a nationally seen TV show. We had fun doing the show and I thought it would be interesting for you, the reader, to see how the process works and the show is finally aired.

What I am referring to is the TV show on the Discovery Channel called "A Haunting." It presently airs on the Discovery Channel on Friday's at 10:00PM, EST. The show is about "real" hauntings that are occurring in people's homes and businesses. What we like about the show is that they don't exaggerate and make the activity so unbelievable that it is hard for the viewer to believe that the activity is actually happening. What you see on the show really happened to the people and that again is what made the show attractive to us.

For those of you that haven't seen the show yet I will try to give you the breakdown of how the show is presented. The show starts out by giving a brief glimpse of the family and the activity they are experiencing. In between the re-enacting and commercials, the real life homeowners will give you a running narrative of their experiences. During the show you will hear the people's voices again recounting some of the events that happened in their house or business.

We found out during the whole process that the real homeowners are not the ones that are doing the re-enactment that you will see on TV. The production company is based in Virginia and they actually have a huge sound stage on a back lot, complete with models of houses for exterior and interior shots. The production company has their own wardrobe department and they are going to "re-create" our shirts so they will be worn during the show. The production company then will hire actors to portray us and the homeowners. I asked to have Brad Pitt play me but was told that their budget wasn't that high. They take the tape from the interview they did with us and transcribe it to paper, from that the script for the show will be made. From the time the interview takes place until you see the finished show on TV, usually about 4-5 months will have passed.

Let me tell you how the whole process started. Charles received an e-mail from a production company looking for stories for a show called "A Haunting." They wanted to know if Charles had any interesting stories that they might be able to use. Charles then forwarded that information to us on December 7, 2005. I then sent an e-mail to Joanne at the production company to find out what kind of story they were looking for. Joanne said they were looking for good and true paranormal stories. The scarier the story the better your chances were of getting approval and begin the taping.

The first investigation that came into my mind that would work perfectly for the show was ironically our first house investigation. It had happened years ago and some of the details were faint at best. We contacted the homeowners from the investigation we had thought of first to see if they would be interested in doing the show. Because without their approval and being onboard with the project any possibility of doing the show would have came to a sudden and complete stop. They said that they would be happy to have their story told and they were excited about the whole thing.

I got back to Joanne and told her that the homeowners were excited about this and I gave her their contact number so she could contact them and discuss the show.

During this process we had to give Joanne all the details concerning the case. The homeowners had to recall everything that happened to them over five years ago.

Then we waited while Joanne wrote the rough draft of the story line and waited for approval from the Discovery Channel. That final approval came on February 9, 2006. Joanne called us to give us the good news and I asked Joanne what would happen next. She said that a crew would come out and interview us. She wanted to know what date in February would work for us, the 24th, 25th or 26th. We told Joanne that we had to check our schedule and that we would get back with her. We looked at our schedule and the only date we could do the interview was on the 26th of February. We e-mailed Joanne with the date we could do the interviews and later we received a e-mail confirmation from Joanne for February 26th, 2006. We were told that they would get to our house at about 10:00 AM EST.

They arrived at promptly 10:00 AM EST. There were three members of the crew. Ray was the onsite director, Greg was in charge of the camera and the shooting angles, and Brian was the sound man. They were really nice people and we got along with them really well. That made the whole experience a really nice one.

We sat with Ray and he discussed with us how the day would pan out. There were three of us left from the original team that did the investigation so we would be the ones being interviewed. I was the first one to be interviewed, followed by Brenda, and last but not least Mary, who has been a member from almost the beginning and joined the group when all we done were cemeteries. My interview would last 1 ½ hours, Brenda and Mary each would have 1 hour each for their interviews. The homeowners from this investigation had their interviews the day before us at a different location. I believe it was in the Detroit area someplace.

We sat on a chair facing the camera. Ray was right in front of the camera, but not in view. Ray would ask us questions concerning the investigation. Things like what we did, how we felt, what equipment we used. The reason for these questions wasn't because he was nosey and wanted to know everything. It was because they were doing an hour show on the investigation that we did. They weren't there and had no idea what transpired during the time spent in the house during the investigation. All the things that we said were going to be transcribed onto paper, and then made into the script. From this script would be the lines that the actors that were portraying us and the homeowners would use for the taping.

So like I mentioned before, Ray was just in front of the camera, out of view, and he would be asking us these questions. If he wanted to clarify an answer he would tell us to use this wording or be a little clearer on that answer and he would ask the question again. He asked us not to move, itch, or scratch too much during the taping. He said that when he talked that part wouldn't see the light of day, in other words it wouldn't make the show, so if we needed to move a little, itch, whatever, when he was talking was the time to do that.

All three interviews went just like this. They did the interview and then spent the next 1-1 ½ hours setting up the next shot. Greg was in charge of getting everything right from the angle of the shot to the props used. This man is a genius. We have seen all of the "A Haunting" shows and you would never know that the interview was conducted in a home. Some of the props that he used for our shoot were some of our equipment, a fan, a candle, and those big colored sheets that look like saran wrap.

Brian was the sound man. His only job was to make sure that we all could be heard on camera and that we were all loud and clear. But then on occasion he would have to stop the interview because a particular loud car was driving by or someone who likes to blast music from their car stereo would drive by also. The sound equipment that he used was so sensitive that before the interview started we needed to unplug the refrigerator and the filter to Rocky's tank, our son's turtle. When the interview was over and they would set up for the next shot we would plug everything back in again. He let us put his headphones on once and you wouldn't believe what noises you could pick up. Motley, our cat, decided she wanted to be petted. The whole house was quiet and she starts purring. I could even hear it but Brian said that it was fine since the microphone stand was next to the person being interviewed and it was in the next room.

The whole day lasted 9 ½ hours. All of this for just a one hour show. But it was all worth it in the end when the show finally aired on the Discovery Channel.

So that in a nutshell was what happened from start to finish. We would like to thank the people at the production company and the onsite crew for making this whole experience such much fun. Not everyone gets to see the process it takes to get a show on the air. I hope this gave you a little taste of the things that we went through to get our story on the air. On the next few pages I have included pictures of the shoot. Enjoy.

Pictures from Our "Shoot"

Camera, lighting, and accessories used during the
Discovery Channel's taping for "A Haunting."

More of the equipment used by the Discovery Channel to film the TV show "A Haunting."

This is Greg from the Discovery Channel's show "A Haunting." Greg was responsible for lighting, the camera angle and props used for the filming of the interviews used for the TV show "A Haunting."

Sound equipment used by the sound man during the filming of the interviews to be used in the Discovery Channel's "A Haunting."

The first 12 years of the existence of SEMGHS has been really interesting. We have met some nice people along the way.

We would like to thank every home and business owner that have allowed us into their homes and businesses over all these years to conduct investigations for paranormal activity! Without you there would be no SEMGHS. We would also like to thank all former and current members of SEMGHS. You have helped make what the group what it is today. Here is to another 12 years. We hope to help as many families as we can in the years to come. I sincerely hope you have enjoyed reading this book.